# PERSONAL
# POLITICS
## THE PSYCHOLOGY OF MAKING IT

# PERSONAL
# POLITICS

## THE PSYCHOLOGY OF MAKING IT

**ELLEN J. LANGER**

*Yale University*

**CAROL S. DWECK**

*University of Illinois*

PRENTICE-HALL, INC., Englewood Cliffs, New Jersey

*Library of Congress Cataloging in Publication Data*

LANGER, ELLEN J.
 Personal politics.

 Includes bibliographies.
 1. Success. 2. Interpersonal relations. I. Dweck,
Carol S., joint author. II. Title.
BF637.S8L35     158′.1     72-12521
ISBN 0-13-657254-5
ISBN 0-13-657247-2 (pbk.)

© 1973 by Ellen J. Langer and Carol S. Dweck

PRINTED IN THE UNITED STATES OF AMERICA

10  9  8  7  6  5  4  3  2  1

Prentice-Hall International, Inc., *London*
Prentice-Hall of Australia, Pty. Ltd., *Sydney*
Prentice-Hall of Canada Ltd., *Toronto*
Prentice-Hall of India Private Limited, *New Delhi*
Prentice-Hall of Japan, Inc., *Tokyo*

*TO SYL AND NORM*

# CONTENTS

Contents

# ACKNOWLEDGMENTS

We would like to extend our most sincere thanks to our friends, colleagues, and mentors who contributed their time and wisdom to the growth of this book and its authors:

To Robert Abelson, Irving Janis, William Kessen, Robert Silverman, Joan Gay Snodgrass, and Allan Wagner who helped to shape our thinking over the past few years. We would like to offer special thanks to those of them who advised us on different aspects of the book.

To Carol Marcus, Shelley Taylor, and Sharon Gurwitz, for making many useful comments on the first version of the manuscript and for laughing in all the appropriate places.

To Edward Lugenbeel, Psychology Editor of Prentice-Hall, for his support and encouragement through all stages of the project, and to Barbara Christenberry, of the College Book Editorial Dept. of Prentice-Hall, for her fine editorial work.

To each other for making this collaborative effort such a rewarding experience.

# PERSONAL
# POLITICS
## THE PSYCHOLOGY OF MAKING IT

# INTRODUCTION

By observing hundreds of people in homes, offices, schools, and social gatherings, we have been forced to conclude that the great majority of Americans are frustrated and unhappy. This isn't true for *all* of the people *all* of the time. Unfortunately, it is true for too many of the people too much of the time.

Some of these people believe that any thinking, feeling person living in times like ours could not possibly be happy, and anyone who is must be shallow or callous. Others believe that happiness is in some way sprinkled upon us by divine dispensation, befalling some but not others. Then there are those who feel that they cannot be really happy without that *one* thing they do not possess, be it wealth, an important job or a certain person.

Few, however, consider the possibility that one can *learn* to be happy. We are proposing a somewhat quick, somewhat easy way to achieve this end. Some of you may be muttering under your breath "Haven't we met someplace before?" Yes, maybe in theory but probably not in practice. While similar claims have been made in the past, rarely has the reader been given specific techniques for putting the suggested ideas into use.

While our approach may result in some important changes, it does not require a radical alteration in life style—no pilgrimage to India with the Maharishi or drastically new diet of crunchy granola and goat's milk yogurt (although we find the first interesting and the second tasty). Moreover, the only elaborate apparatus required is your head.

We will try to teach you how to apply principles derived from psychological research to common personal and interpersonal situations—from intimate sexual behavior to public social encounters—in a way that is hopefully both entertaining and meaningful. Many of the principles we will discuss (e.g., principles of reinforcement) are ones you already use—but not with maximum precision and effectiveness. Some of the strategies we will suggest (e.g., searching for alternatives) are ones you may be familiar with—but do not carry far enough. We will present more powerful ways of requesting, giving, or picking up information. We will question things you may take for granted and faulty assumptions you never bothered to examine.

The goal is to increase your level of awareness by having you examine your approach to situations, by making you skillful in obtaining and using information, and by emphasizing the *control* you have over yourself and your environment.

We will not stress insight into the origins of one's difficulties, for insight, while nice, is not enough. Take the example of the woman who has trouble relating to men. She may learn, correctly or incorrectly, that this affliction stems from her relationship with her father during her early years. She may feel wonderful for the moment at having made this "discovery." But how does this insight prepare her for the future? In order to avoid the recurrence of frustrating experiences she still has to learn and practice new ways of relating to men.

Specific problem situations like this will be presented in the form of scenarios or case studies, alternative views of the situation will be discussed, and specific recommendations and behavioral techniques will be provided for dealing with the difficulty. The techniques have been extensively tested and have been found to be most effective.

However, in order for them to work for you, you must think of the particular examples in your own life where what we have said may be true, and then, it is most important to try the suggestions out. The better you are at generalizing from our particular examples to your particular situations, the more helpful this book will be. In short, we hope that you will find the reading enjoyable, the implementation fun, and the consequences rewarding.

# *Status Woe*

## EXPLANATIONS FOR UNHAPPINESS

Let's now consider some of the reasons why people may remain in a state of discontent *despite* efforts to change their condition. These reasons fall into four fundamental categories: the inability to find adequate explanations for unhappiness; the inability to persuade others of the merits of our arguments; the inability to search for alternative explanations for events we view as unpleasant; the inability to effectively use established principles of control. In the course of the following preview we will explore each of these fundamental categories as well as formulate some of the principles and strategies for change that will be elaborated throughout the book.

### (1) Inability to Find Adequate Explanations

Most people try to find explanations for the way they feel, especially if the feeling is negative—depression, boredom, or anger. The explanation they come up with may suggest to them what to do to dispel the unpleasant feeling. Unfortunately, the reason that is chosen is generally so vague or global that the course of action it leads to, if any, may prove fruitless or destructive.

Often, a prominent characteristic of an individual's life style is blamed for the unhappiness. Marital status may be one such scapegoat. For example, if a person knows he is unhappy *and* married, he may conclude that he is unhappy *because* he is married. Divorce may then seem the appropriate course of action. But he has failed to notice the specific circumstances within and without the marriage which led to this discontent. The conclusion is thus premature and perhaps faulty. What's more, the conclusion may prevent him from looking for more helpful explanations.

Similarly, people often give labels to *themselves* and somehow think that they have then "explained" why they are unhappy. This may consist of taking the adjective that describes how they feel and tacking it on to the word "person"—as in answering the question "Why am I depressed?" with the answer "Because I'm a depressed person," or "Why aren't I motivated?" with "Because I'm an apathetic person." Or, it may consist of isolating a certain area in which they feel they have not succeeded and assigning themselves such labels as "unsociable," "unathletic," or "unartistic." As in the marriage example, the label, which masquerades as explanation, prevents the person from examining the specific incidents and behaviors which led to the application of the label. The strategy that such name-calling seems to suggest is one of resignation, for the names imply deep-seated, unchangeable characteristics. They discourage the individual from engaging in the very activities that might serve to dispel the label.

If someone is unhappy in a relationship, he may assign a label (like dull, cold, or selfish) to the *other* person(s) in order to "explain" why their interaction is unsatisfying. This may absolve him of any responsibility for what their relationship lacks, but it also deprives him of the opportunity to exert his control over the situation. Moreover, he may begin to react to the label rather than the person. For example, James calls his friend Terry "inconsiderate," because she knows nothing and cares less about cars, his great passion. If he does this often enough, then he may begin to respond to Terry as inconsiderate in a variety of instances where the label is uncalled for. This will no doubt have other repercussions in their relationship. Or consider Cynthia who is tremendously impressed by all the famous people that her date knows. Because of her excitement, she decides to take him to meet her friend. The next day on the telephone she asks her friend what she thought of him. Her friend replies, "He's nice, but he's something of a name dropper, don't you think?" Now each time Cynthia hears him refer to his famous friends (usually just the way she would refer to her own friends) she is annoyed rather than impressed. For her, the label "name dropper" has turned a virtue into a vice.

Pseudoexplanations and unflattering labels may make problems where there are none or obscure otherwise obvious solutions.

### (2) Inability to Persuade

Do people disagree with you because your points are invalid or because they are not well taken? Pause for a moment before answering this question and try to recall the last time you *unsuccessfully* attempted to convince somebody of something—whether you should go out for Chinese or Italian food, why they should stop that annoying habit of eating in bed or cracking their knuckles, how they should dress, or whom they should vote for in the next election.

Returning to the original question—"Do people disagree with you because your points are invalid or because they are not well taken?"—it is not difficult to see how either answer might result in unhappiness, self-condemnation, or resentment. If you came away feeling your points were invalid, you may well have felt

7

inadequate. If you came away believing your argument was sound but not well received, you may have felt that the other party was stupid or stubborn.

Instead of asking "Was I wrong (or stupid)?" or "Was he wrong (or stupid)?" a more productive approach, and one which stresses your control, would be to ask, "Do people disagree with me because my points are not put across as effectively as they might be?"

Stu would like to persuade Phil to stop eating a certain food for his own good. He takes the next opportunity available to try to get his point across.

> "Say Phil, you'd better not eat fruit crunchies any more. They think the XPQ in them causes cancer."

> "Come on Stu, every day they call something else dangerous. It's all a lot of political bull."

Obviously, Phil is not convinced. Had Stu only thought in advance about how his friend would react to a message like that, he probably could have been more persuasive. This is not as difficult as it may sound. Because Stu has heard Phil's responses to similar statements in the past, and people tend to be consistent, he can now venture a good guess as to what his friend's reaction will be this time. Then, with Phil's probable reaction in mind, Stu could have phrased the message so as to disclaim Phil's objection in advance: "Phil, I know every day they say that another one of our favorite foods is no good, but this time it's not a lot of political bull. They think the XPQ . . ."

We all know which of our friends will think a certain statement is superstition, which will think it represents a sexist, communist, or fascist ploy, or which will believe it at face value. For those who will be resistent, one method, then, of heading off the "yes, but . . ." is by preceding your statement with a disclaimer.

> "I hope this won't get you angry, but . . ."

> "I know this may sound ridiculous, but . . ." etc.

This will not always work—but then again, nothing does. There are, however, instances where it is more likely to work than not. We will go into these cases later when we elaborate other persuasion techniques.

A second and, for the time being, the last persuasion strategy concerns the phrasing of questions. Often people are disappointed because their question did not elicit the answer they had hoped for. They mistakenly assume that asking a question is like putting a penny into a bubble gum machine. No matter how you put the question, the answer will still be the same. This line of reasoning assumes that the answer is either 1) formulated before the question is asked, or 2) formulated on the spot, but is not affected by the question. On many occasions, however, the phrasing of the question may actually determine the answer— especially when the person has not quite made up his mind.

> Beth is eager to see the new movie *Away with the Draft* (the low budget remake of *Gone with the Wind*). She is hoping Bart will take her. When he comes for dinner, she says, "You don't want to go to the movies do you?" Since Bart rarely wants to do anything until he's doing it, he says, "No."
>
> Perhaps if she had said, "It's okay if we go to the movies tonight, isn't it?" it would have been harder for him to refuse.
>
> Michael, a convivial host, would like his friends to continue drinking, but he has only one bottle of liquor left. He decides he'll keep asking his guests "Would you like another drink?" until the liquor runs out. If he asked, "Have you had enough to drink?" the bottle would probably have lasted much longer.

### (3) Inability to Search for Positive Alternatives

Well-intentioned relatives, the mass media, and children's books trained many of us in childhood to look at the world in black/white terms, rarely mentioning all the shades of gray. There were the good or the bad guys, the big or the small, the shoulds or should nots. The moderates, mediums, sometimes, and maybes were virtually eliminated for fear they would be confusing. And how many times in school did the teacher go around the room in search of *the* right answer?

As adults we've experienced that gray in-between area often enough to understand that the either/or reasoning was often faulty. However more than just a vestige of that past remains.

Many of us still tend to look for the *one* right answer or explanation, so when we find *any* explanation that seems to fit the question asked, we end our search. This explanation is then seen as *the* right answer, and all others by definition become wrong. But it is all too frequent that these explanations are of other people's motives, intentions, or thoughts—all of which are *private* events. As such, we have no way of ever being sure whether our interpretation is indeed correct.

Why should you continue to search for alternative explanations when you have found one that seems to fit? The answer is simple—in order to alleviate or prevent the frustrations you often encounter. This may best be appreciated as an analogy to the bet on God's existence as stated by the French philosopher, Pascal.

Pascal proposed that we look at the possibility of God's existence as a gambler examines a wager. Will an individual be better off by believing or not believing in God? Examine the possibilities before placing your bet since this will serve as a paradigm for later.

**Question:** Is there a God?

**Negative View:** There is no God.

**Consequences:** If I believe that there is no God and there *is no* God, nothing is lost. However, if I believe that there is no God and it turns out that there *is* a God, on "Judgement Day" I've lost everything.

This gamble seems to be too risky. Is there an alternative?

**Positive View:** There is a God.

*Consequences:* If I believe there is a God and it turns out that there *is no* God, then I've lost nothing. However, if I believe that there is a God and it turns out that I'm right that there *is* a God, then I'm in heaven.

By the negative view you can't win and by the positive view you can't lose. It is easy to see that the positive view is then the "best bet."

While we are not really concerned with whether or not you take Pascal's best bet for a "hereafter," we *are* concerned that you stake your bets on our wager for the here and now.

In personal or interpersonal situations a positive interpretation consists of the individual's seeking positive, nonfrustrating

alternatives for his own and others' intentions and behavior. This is not to suggest that the positively oriented person sees the world through rose-colored glasses or lives by a rule of denying the reality. Without distorting reality, he sees all sides but places emphasis on the positive—focusing on the doughnut and not the hole—though both are there. Since nothing is completely bad or negative, it is always possible for him to find a viable alternative.

The negative view of life needs no further explication here. It is well known to each of us, for we all too often give in to it. Yet a positive approach is no more difficult to learn than the negative. The problem is that once you've learned to view the world and yourself negatively, it requires some practice to make the transition.

> *Fact:* Heedlock Aircraft Corporation is forced to make cuts in the number of aeronautical engineers they employ. George is an aeronautical engineer. F. Peterson Heedlock III, George's boss, lately has not been speaking to George as often as he used to. In the past, Heedlock frequently stopped by George's office to chat about the progress George was making on his current project.
>
> George's negative interpretation of these facts went as follows:
>
> *Negative View:* "After all this hard work, that bastard is going to fire me." (A watered down version to be sure!)
>
> *Consequences:* If he interprets Heedlock's aloof manner as an indication that he is going to lose his job and he is right, he has lost nothing more than his job.
>
> If he believes he is going to be fired and this was not at all what Heedlock had intended, George might not continue to work with the same motivation and standards as before and would thereby increase the likelihood of fulfilling his own prophecy—certainly a losing proposition.
>
> *Positive View:* "I don't think I'm going to be fired, 'something else' probably explains the change in Heedlock's behavior; Maybe Heedlock's uptight about the company's financial crisis; Heedlock isn't coming around so the other men won't think I'm keeping

my job because of a personal friendship rather than good work; Or perhaps Heedlock hasn't been feeling well lately;" etc.

*Consequences:* If George assumes that he isn't going to be fired and he is to be fired, then he may be able to take with him a better recommendation for having continued his good work to the end. Or he may even change Heedlock's mind, despite the crisis, because of his good work. At worst, George loses no more as a result of his views.

Keep in mind that by taking this view, George is not denying the possibility that he may be fired. Thus he is not prevented from protecting himself by keeping his eyes open for other jobs.

If, however, George takes the positive view, that "something else" (other than imminent loss of job) may explain Heedlock's behavior and indeed he is correct, then he wins and has saved himself all that agonizing.

Once again the best bet is clear.

Focusing on positives rather than negatives will result in payoffs in all areas. Take the interaction between a husband and wife below as another illustration.

*Fact:* Don sees Arlene talking to his boss at a big party. She is laughing and smiling much more than usual. Don's boss happens to be both very handsome and very single.

*Negative View:* Don assumes that Arlene is *flirting* with the handsomest man at the party.

*Consequences:* When Arlene returns to Don's side he is somewhat nasty while he attempts to keep his jealousy in check. Arlene gets annoyed at him because of all the obnoxious things he says while in this state. Don interprets this annoyance as evidence that she would rather be with his boss than with him. They go home to fight.

*Positive View:* Don assumes that Arlene is lapping up all of his boss's old jokes and stories so that she will make a good impression and thereby help him to advance in the firm.

**Consequences:** When Arlene returns to Don's side he is appreciative and sweeter than ever. If his guess was right, Arlene will respond to his good mood with affection. If she was indeed flirting, she'll probably now feel badly about it, appreciate Don's understanding and therefore respond affectionately. In either case, Don and Arlene now go home to make love.

### (4) Inability to Use Principles of Control and Recognize Your Power

Every time someone smiles, nods, frowns, or snickers at us they are controlling our behavior. The next chapter explains how.

# T W O

## *Power to the People*

### THE POLITICS OF CONTROL

Does the thought of being manipulated frighten you? People often conjure up the image of a malevolent tyrant suppressing the freedom of his helpless subjects, commanding them to think thoughts and commit acts against their will. The picture is one of a society where the innocence of children is sacrificed as they are forced into preordained molds:

"Put them down on the floor."

The infants were unloaded.

"Now turn them so that they can see the flowers and books."

Turned, the babies at once fell silent, then began to crawl towards those clusters of sleek colours, those shapes so gay and brilliant on the white pages. . . .

The director waited until all were happily busy. Then, "Watch carefully," he said. And, lifting his hand, he gave the signal.

The Head Nurse, who was standing by a switchboard at the other end of the room, pressed down a little lever.

There was a violent explosion. Shriller and ever shriller, a siren shrieked. Alarm bells maddingly sounded. . . .

"And now," the Director shouted (for the noise was deafening), "now we proceed to rub in the lesson with a mild electric shock."*

And so Huxley continues to relate how some infants of his *Brave New World* were conditioned to avoid flowers and books. Nature and culture did not fit in with the plans that the state had for these children, for they would distract them from their prescribed duties as adults.

Was Huxley exaggerating the power of behavioral technology? No. Over and over, results of experimental work done in psychological laboratories have demonstrated the degree to which the behavior of both man and animal is subject to control. We hardly think the human condition will reach the state depicted by Huxley. Nevertheless, there *is* a science of behavior. The danger lies not in its existence, but in the denial of its reality. It may be a powerful weapon if left in the hands of a few, but when it is common property it becomes man's most useful tool for enhancing personal fulfillment.

"Control" and "manipulation" are words whose connotations have come to obscure their meanings. When we say a person is manipulative, we often imply that he engages in deception for his own gain. If the same act is performed when deception is absent and/or gain is not apparent, we no longer call it manipulation. We might call the former calculating and the latter thoughtful, although both are forms of control.

But let's look more closely at the different types of control and manipulation and see how people generally react to them. First we'll consider cases in which people might consider the motive or outcome of the control to be negative. Then we'll con-

* From Aldous Huxley, *Brave New World* (New York: Harper & Row, 1968), pp. 12–13.

sider cases in which people would consider the motive or outcome to be positive, even though the manipulation may be just
as powerful. We will ask the questions: Do we reject manipulation and control per se or do we reject them only in certain con-
texts? Do we really have the choice of rejecting them? Can we
afford to fool ourselves into thinking we have the choice?

It is not surprising that the thought of manipulation is offensive in view of the many politicians trying to win our votes with
hollow promises of peace and prosperity, high-pressure salesmen
convincing us that we need a second set of encyclopedias, and
Madison Avenue ad men sending women off to buy midiskirts,
and men to buy Nehru jackets. This kind of manipulation is
often met with anger and resentment because we attribute selfish motives to these agents; we end up with something we didn't
want and we feel we've been had. Many of us remember when
"Buy popcorn" messages were subliminally flashed on our movie
screens and how the public responded with fear and apprehen-
sion. Again they may have felt that they had fallen prey to some
money-monger's acquisitive instincts.

In addition, there are many situations in which the attempt
to control is seen as unintentional, although here we don't usually use the word manipulation. People may force others into
situations which have negative consequences without "meaning
to." When this "unintentional" control is blatant, it is usually
forgiven; when it is subtle, most people remain unaware of the
fact that it has taken place.

But people often try to get other people to do things for positive reasons and with positive outcomes. For example, we are
urging you to read this book in the belief that you will gain from
this investment of your time and energy. Think of a person
primping and preening for an hour and a half to impress a date,
a wife cooking a great dinner before showing her husband her
new Pucci's and Gucci's, the boss giving you a raise because of
your smashing success with the new client—none of these would
be considered reprehensible and yet they are just as "manipulative" as our first examples. It is clear that the context determines

our judgment; we reject the idea of control in some situations but not in others. But even the attempts of our politicians, salesmen, ad men and popcorn flashers need not be met with fear, anger, or resentment if we understand what control is and how it works.

Virtually all situations, personal and interpersonal, contain elements of control—whether you realize it or not. Saying that the idea of control "turns me off" doesn't make this go away. Rather, it leaves situations to chance and paves the way for results that may be to nobody's satisfaction. Specifying the desired outcomes and acknowledging your power of control in reaching those outcomes allows you to view the notion of "fate" as a meaningless construct formulated by the underdog:

> . . . Miniver Cheevy born too late
> Scratched his head and kept on thinking;
> Miniver coughed and called it fate,
> And kept on drinking.
>
> E. A. ROBINSON (1910)*

## A Matter of Principle and A Principle of Matter

How does control operate? You tell your friend that you love her chocolate cake more than anything in the world, and, lo and behold, you find another chocolate cake waiting for you on your next visit. You use a certain line for openers: "Was it Tangier?" and if it works you use it when the occasion presents itself again. When you reveal a fascinating story about yourself, people sit up and listen. This new found interest in you is so flattering that you continue to disclose chapters of your life. You are polite and friendly to the hassled waiter. He gives you better service. You

* Four lines from "Miniver Cheevy" (Copyright 1907 Charles Scribner's Sons; renewal copyright 1935) are reprinted by permission of Charles Scribner's Sons from *The Town Down the River* by Edwin Arlington Robinson.

give him a bigger tip. He gives other customers better service. You are more pleasant to other waiters.

In each case the action was followed by a positive consequence. Since people seek out positive consequences, the action is more likely to be repeated. This process is known as positive reinforcement (or reward). In principle it is very simple: If an action is followed by a pleasant event, the likelihood of the action's recurring is increased.

The control is reciprocal. While your compliment rewarded her cake baking, her cakes rewarded your complimenting. In the same way, people's attentive listening rewarded your disclosing information about yourself, and your further disclosures rewarded their attentive listening. The waiter example speaks for itself.

*"They never pushed me. If I wanted to retrieve, shake hands, or roll over, it was entirely up to me."*

Drawing by Frascino; © 1971 The New Yorker Magazine, Inc.

Unfortunately, *the reward* doesn't know whether the behavior it is rewarding is desirable or not. In the above examples the rewarded behaviors were for the most part desirable. However, it is important to understand that undesirable behavior also increases

19

in likelihood when it is followed by pleasant consequences. A child steals money, and, if not discovered, he is more likely to steal again and again, for each time his stealing is rewarded by the stolen object. One partner behaves like a tyrant, and the other submits and caters to his (her) demands—the tyrannical behavior may be sustained or escalated. If the only time you're affectionate or complimentary is when your mate threatens to leave you, then the threats are more likely to occur. With these examples in mind, you may better understand why people behave in undesirable ways such as stealing, bitching, fighting. They may also lead you to examine your relationships and beware that you do not reward the very behaviors you'd like to eliminate.

While the principle of reinforcement is quite simple, the lack of surface complexity does not reflect a limited applicability. The number of behaviors that are instituted and maintained in this manner is multitudinous.

Most people will accept the fact that knowledge is power, whether it is knowing how to land a job, being the life of the party, or knowing your way around the bedroom. A firm understanding of the principles of reinforcement and a few other behavioral laws to be explained in a moment will equip you with the knowledge to give you the powers you desire.


### *Always, Sometimes, Never: Schedules of Reinforcement*

While you probably don't need psychologists to tell you that you can get people to do things by offering them rewards, the most effective ways of offering these rewards are less obvious.

Jim has been calling and asking both Andrea and Carrie to go out. Carrie has always accepted his invitations while Andrea has accepted less frequently. Assuming he likes them both equally well, whom would you predict that he would stop calling first if both girls began to refuse him consistently?

You may reinforce a behavior each time it occurs, or you may reinforce it only occasionally. These strategies are technically known as schedules—continuous reinforcement schedules and intermittent reinforcement schedules. The important thing to know about all of this is that the different schedules determine how the behavior will continue after the reward has stopped. Behavior reinforced on an intermittent schedule (i.e., only sometimes) is more resistant to extinction (will continue longer) than behavior reinforced on a continuous schedule. Therefore, it is Andrea's phone that will continue ringing after Carrie's has stopped.

To further illustrate this point, consider a nagging child. If you let the child interrupt your conversation (child's interruptions rewarded by attention) every so often and then decided never to let him interrupt again, the child would continue interrupting for a fairly long period of time, even though his attempts were unsuccessful. However, if you gave in to every one of the child's outbursts and then decided never to give in again, the child would stop interrupting after fewer unsuccessful tries—it would be clear that the rules of the game had changed.

As an important aside, we should mention two factors that might stand in the way of eliminating this annoying behavior. One is the fact that when you begin to ignore the child, his efforts will be stepped up (he'll wail more loudly and tug at you harder). This happens whenever you stop rewarding (i.e., extinguish) something you had formerly rewarded. If you are serious about eliminating the interruptions, the only solution is to answer the child's persistence with your own persistence, for if you gave in now, you'd be reinforcing this more vehement form of intrusion. The second and closely related factor, is that the child is controlling your behavior at the same time you are controlling his. His nagging and tugging annoy you, and when you give him your attention, they cease. The cessation of an annoying stimulus is also reinforcing (technically called negative reinforcement) and as such, maintains the behavior leading to it.

21

### IS A PENNY SAVED, A PENNY EARNED?

Ralph and Penny are vacationing in Las Vegas. They are on their way to dinner when Penny decides to detour to the ladies room. Ralph, with a few minutes to kill, spots the slot machines a few feet away. Although he has proclaimed himself a nongambler, he becomes more and more intrigued. He slowly sneaks over to the "deadly toys," inserts a quarter into the enticing one-arm bandit, and pulls the lever. He loses. He surreptitiously reaches into his pocket for another coin and deposits it into the machine. Jackpot. This time his lever press is rewarded with the return of six shining new quarters. He quickly and excitedly inserts another coin. Nothing happens. He tries again; nothing happens. Again and again—but nothing happens. He gradually returns to his old pace—depositing the coin rather slyly and slowly pulling the lever. He loses again. With one last coin in his hand, Ralph "decides" to feed the box one more time and walk away rather than dip into his pocket for a new supply of money. Jackpot. Four quarters spill out. His enthusiasm is once again restored. In goes another coin, up pops a lemon, a bell, a plum, but no money comes out.

Penny, now ready to dine, searches for her husband. She is soon to find him—in a rather embarrassing state for a nongambler. He gives her an affectionate kiss with an excuse and tells her he'll be only a minute longer. It was a minute longer, longer than any other she had ever spent. He won occasionally, but now his losses were starting to cost him his own money. Did Ralph stay at the machine all night? Of course not. Because he wasn't "really" a gambler? No, he left in order to avoid a battle with his wife and to go see Barbara Streisand, who was singing across the street.

The next day, while Ralph is outside swimming, Penny decides to see if that slot machine was exciting enough to explain the fight she and Ralph had the night before. She puts in her quarter —up shoot three bells and out pour six quarters. She puts in another coin and out come four more quarters. In goes another coin and out come five quarters. Her fourth attempt is unsuccessful. So are her fifth, sixth, and seventh (still far fewer tries than Ralph). She returns to the poolside thinking that the machine was fun, but a little boring.

Is Ralph a foolish hypocrite while Penny is so controlled and sensible? Maybe so, but this little excerpt from their story in no way provides evidence for that assertion. More accurately, the different schedules of reinforcement that were operative dictated their behavior.

Does this mean that we are mere victims of schedules? Not if we are both aware of and willing to exert the control we do have. Awareness of the relationship between your behavior and its outcomes will not in itself change the controlling forces. That is, even if Ralph knew that he was on an intermittent schedule of reinforcement, or if Penny knew that she was on a continuous schedule of reinforcement, they would still have behaved as they did. What *will* change the relationship is the introduction of new variables into the situation.

By this we mean new factors that will compete with the slot machine for his attention. They may consist of more attractive alternatives, or of highly aversive consequences, or a combination of the two. In Ralph's case the main competing factors were the attraction of the Barbara Streisand concert and the avoidance of a fight with Penny. It was just a lucky accident that these other factors intervened to keep him from risking a small fortune. However, had Ralph intended to gamble and been aware of the risk involved, he could have set limits for himself in advance and taken measures to insure that he'd stick to them.

When viewed from afar it might seem that such measures are unnecessary if the person involved only had some "self-control." But what is self-control in the face of temptation if not the availability of more powerful competing alternatives? People have the opportunity to control themselves by intentionally programming the more desirable alternatives. Self-control is in principle no different from other forms of control. In the case of gambling, one may set time limits by arranging other engagements you are eager to keep (e.g., make a date with an attractive person, purchase tickets for a show, etc.) and which begin some fixed time after you enter the casino.

Another method of exercising self-control is by making a public commitment to some individual or group whose opinion you value and whose respect you desire. This would consist of openly stating the course of action you plan to take. It is effective because by violating your commitment you run the risk of losing credibility and face. Avoidance of these negative consequences may add the extra motivation to do what you initially wanted to do anyway.

How else might the gambler keep from losing his shirt? He may limit the amount of money he brings with him in the first place. This will then enable him to leave the situation as soon as the chosen amount of money runs out.

Gambling is by no means the only situation where the issue of self-control arises. Self-control or "will power" is important in any instance in which an individual is not sure that he will do what's "good for him" in the long run.

The point to be understood now, however, is that reinforcement contingencies are powerful, but need not be overpowering. You can introduce new factors into the controlling relationships and thereby preserve what you might regard as your freedom and dignity.

## All that Glitters Is Not Goals

In order to use reinforcements effectively, you must first clearly define your goal. People often set goals that sound lofty and admirable but are impossible to attain because of the lack of precision. The more specifically you define your goal in terms of *overt behaviors*, the easier it is to achieve.

Ann regards her roommate, Leslie, as lazy. Her diagnosis has led to the strategy of nagging and complaining. Leslie, however, has not responded well to this form of "therapy." Ann would have been more effective had she 1) clearly defined the specific tasks she wished Leslie to perform, and 2) found the way to motivate Leslie to perform them. Her goal may include any or all of the following tasks—making the bed, doing all the dishes, or putting away all of the clothes after doing the laundry. She should proceed towards the goal in small, discrete steps. When the defined behavior or an approximation of that behavior (e.g., some, instead of all, of the dishes) is performed, Ann should immediately follow it with reward. The reward may be praise, a thank you, or perhaps a promise to do something in return like make a delicious dinner —anything that works. A behavior resulting in a pleasant outcome is likely to be repeated, and so Leslie is on the way to becoming unlazy.

## *Punishment*

Control can be achieved by either rewarding the desired behavior or by punishing undesired behavior. An employer can get his workers to increase production by administering rewards like praise or money, if they do work harder, or punishments like reprimands, warnings, or docking salary if they don't.

As a general rule we would advocate the use of positive control with rewards rather than negative control through the use of punishment. While both means of control may be effective in the short run, the effectiveness of punishment is often only temporary. In fact, when the punishment is discontinued, the formerly punished behavior may occur at an even higher rate than before. Moreover, punishment can have unwanted emotional side effects. We are including a discussion of punishment, however, because we wish to point out how people often punish the very behaviors they wish to promote.

"If only she were the kind of person who liked parties." Ted is annoyed and frustrated at the "fact" that his wife, Sara, is "unsociable." This is a facile and blinding explanation of why Sara avoids parties and argues with Ted each time he urges her to attend. "Sociability" is made up of learned responses which can be rewarded or punished like other learned responses. The question that must be asked is what is maintaining Sara's negative reaction to social gatherings.

Perhaps it's the fact that no sooner do they leave a party than Ted gives her a detailed description of every mistake she made during the evening—how she contradicted him in public, flirted with Arnie Jason, unintentionally insulted Sam Barrett, etc. Since criticism is so distasteful to Sara she avoids this punishment by avoiding parties altogether.

Whenever someone approaches or avoids a situation, there are controlling influences. They may be obvious, as in the case above, or subtle so that closer scrutiny is required. In either case, however, you must isolate these factors in order to control them.

Suppose Sara doesn't stop avoiding parties when Ted's criticism stops, then that was not the controlling force. He must look for subtler influences. Maybe she doesn't enjoy drinking or smoking and is made to feel foolish. Or perhaps parties are aversive because they are usually given on Saturday night when her favorite program is on television. Perhaps when Ted dresses for parties he looks particularly attractive, but gives Sara the "look but don't touch 'til later" look. And after the party when Sara's tired of looking and ready to touch, Ted is honestly just too tired.

By labeling Sara "unsociable," Ted was prevented from seeing the connection between his behavior and Sara's avoidance of parties. Now that he is aware of the relationship he can try to end Sara's avoidance behavior by eliminating the unpleasant consequences of party-going. He can do this in conjunction with rewarding the desirable, in this case "sociable," behavior. That is, besides eliminating the punishments that were keeping the behavior from occurring (insulting and the like), Ted might also compliment the way she looked, relate nice things that were said about her, be more attentive at parties—praise all the things he thinks she did well.

We have illustrated just a few examples of the many ways in which people exert control over each other through the use of rewards and punishments. We hope that these examples have demonstrated that control is not a mysterious entity to be feared, but, rather, it is a necessary element of personal politics. The impact of the principles of control that we have reviewed will be fully appreciated, however, only when you test them out. We can only repeat the recommendation of the old man who, when stopped on the street and asked, "How do you get to Carnegie Hall?" replied, "Practice."

You may be thinking human behavior is so complex that such a simple principle couldn't possibly explain why we act the way we do. Human behavior is indeed complex—but complexity is not the issue. The point is that no matter how simple or elaborate the behavior is, it is affected by its consequences. If the consequences are positive, the behavior will be repeated; if the consequences are negative, it may not.

Do positive and negative consequences have the same meaning for all people? Aren't there some people who don't give up in the face of continued adversity? Aren't there others who surrender the minute something goes wrong? Is the difference simply that the persevering person was on an intermittent schedule of reinforcement, and the giver-upper was on a continuous one? Not really. Between the time that an event occurs and the time we react to it, very often something intervenes. We interpret what has taken place. And just as different people have learned to behave in different ways, so too have they learned to interpret events differently. In the next chapter we will discuss the different ways in which people view positive and negative events. We will explain how these views influence their subsequent behavior.

# THREE

# I Think I Am, Therefore I Am

## SELF-CONCEPT

Human reason needs only to will more strongly than fate and she
is fate.

THOMAS MANN [*]

Who is it that is free of feelings of insecurity? Is it the rich, the
very bright, the athletic, the actor or comedian, the person that
you envy the most? We maintain that there are few, if any, of
us who have a truly satisfying self-concept. People occasionally
put on a good show and seem to others to be on top of it all, but
these very same people often think: "If they only knew the real
me."

We see others with their public faces on, and we are usually
not permitted to view the feelings of inadequacy that lurk be-
neath. Thus we pick up positive information about other people's self-esteem and dwell on the negative information we have
about ourselves. We are bound to suffer by the comparison.

[*] From Thomas Mann, *The Magic Mountain* (New York: Random
House, 1955), p. 381, Modern Library Edition.

Some anecdotal evidence comes from a brief interchange that was recently shared with us. The conversation was between two faculty members of a prestigious university in the East. One of the professors is a member of a minority group and as a result has a great deal of empathy for the minority students. He commented that it was really rough for the men and women coming from the ghettoes to the university because of the feeling that they weren't "really" bright enough. They felt that they were faking it. They faked their way into the school and were therefore fearful that their success would vanish if they let down their masks for more than a moment. The other faculty member was somewhat amazed because it was her belief that these were the students who were most secure. She thought they must be secure because they had a harder fight up the ladder—they must know by now that they are competent. Prior to this conversation her sympathies were basically with the students who were both members of the majority group and wealthy. These were the people who never really had to work for anything. They could never be sure that they could make it on their own—that if "mommy and daddy" weren't around they wouldn't crumble.

Then who is secure? People who recognize their assets and who realize the control they have over their own lives. These are the people who do not see themselves merely as victims or beneficiaries of circumstances.

Many insecure people tend to minimize the role that their true abilities and efforts played in determining success. They tend to emphasize external factors or factors beyond their control and view the successes as somehow unearned or undeserved. Many popular pseudoexplanations feed these myths:

It's not *what* you know but *whom* you know.
He was born with a silver spoon in his mouth.
He had it made, or: He was born under a lucky star.
Either you've got it or you don't.

When applied to yourself, they could be damaging. They lead

one to believe that these are the only factors at work; they make no mention of the individual's beliefs and attitudes about himself and how they contribute to his success. For example, success is often attributed to "connections": Brad thought he got into college because his father knew the dean; Hal thought he was promoted to supervisor because his boss, Catherine, was interested in "getting to know him better." There is *no* accomplishment which a clever enough person can't explain away by finding some extenuating circumstance. But what does this buy you— anxiety because you have to keep up the act or frustration because you're not as good as you think you "should" be? Connections may get you in—but rarely are they enough to keep you in. And what makes you so sure that all those other people made it without help?

By not focusing your attention on the effort you've expended to attain the goal or the clever way *you* brought about the positive consequences, you deny yourself that pat on the back you deserve; the pat on the back we all so desperately need. That is, by attending to external or uncontrollable influences, as suggested in the clichés presented, you may well prevent yourself from attaining a sense of worth.

In a similar way, common statements may masquerade as explanations of failure:

He was cursed from the day he was born.
He was born on the wrong side of the tracks.

Again no mention is made of how a person's belief about his worth contributes to failure when, in fact, this may be a much more important influence than curses or tracks.

We are suggesting an alternative position: You are what you think you are.

Of course, learning is involved in this process. You can't just say "I want to make myself a malted. Poof! I'm a malted!" Phrased differently, our position is: You are what you've learned to be; you view things (including yourself) in the way you've learned to view them. Moreover, you've taught other people how to view you. In the rest of this chapter we will demonstrate how your expectation for yourself can become a self-fulfilling prophecy —how the prediction of failure begets failure and the prediction of success begets success. We will show you how you can change these expectations in order to act in more adaptive ways and bring about more rewarding consequences.

We will then present illustrations of people who may very well sound familiar to you. They are people whose misery stemmed, stems, or will stem from the way they define themselves and compare themselves to others. You'll meet Hank, a resourceful lawyer, who tried on a new self-image and restyled his life, Lucy, a young woman who persistently put herself down and suffered for it; and Roger, who put others down to build himself up and also suffered for it. There will be those whose confidence rests on too narrow a conception of themselves as well as others who cause themselves unnecessary grief because they compare themselves to the wrong people.

## The Virtuous Circle of Success

Some of us are lucky enough to have been trained early to see ourselves in a positive light. As Freud put it: "A man who has been the undisputable favorite of his mother keeps for life the feeling of conqueror, that confidence of success that often induces real success."*

The person who has a high regard for his assets and abilities and who believes he will succeed will act in ways consistent with his expectations. He has learned to make the best bet; that is, he has learned to focus on the positive alternatives. How does this attitude increase the likelihood of success? This may be understood by conceptualizing the process in four stages:

* From Ernest Jones, *Life and Works of Sigmund Freud* (Garden City, N.Y.: Doubleday-Anchor Books, 1963), p. 6, Basic Books Edition.

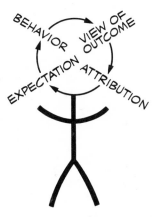

(1) **Expectation.** An individual defines a goal for himself. His expectation refers to how certain he is that he will reach that goal.

> A forty-five year old divorcé, Dennis, is comtemplating having an affair with Marcia, the company's "fresh-out-of-college" research assistant.

Assume for the moment that Dennis expects to be successful in his pursuits.

(2) **Behavior in the Situation.** A person tends to work harder and more consistently when he is fairly certain that his efforts will pay off. Thus an expectation of success will lead to greater effort in the situation, which, of course, will increase the chances of succeeding.

> Because this is the first time Dennis has attempted to date anyone his daughter's age, and he is bent on succeeding, he proceeds with a plan that took him a good deal of time to think out and put into action. He obtains information about the project Marcia is currently working on. After gaining a fair degree of familiarity with the subject matter, he initiates a conversation with her. While strolling through her lab one day, he stops to ask her a few

interesting questions about the research. He begins to make frequent visits with the timing of each visit getting later and later in the day. Surprisingly enough, on Friday he appears at 4:45 and after a short conversation, he asks, "Marcia, if you're not doing anything else, would you like to have dinner with me tonight?"

(3) *View of the Outcome.* This stage involves deciding whether you succeeded or failed by comparing the outcome of the situation to the goal you initially defined for yourself. Often outcomes cannot be clearly labelled "success" or "failure." On such occasions expectations will determine whether you see it one way or the other. In general, an expectation of success makes you more likely to accept the positive alternative and see the outcome as a success. As we showed in the discussion of the "wager" in the introduction, this can maximize the probability of future success.

How did Marcia respond to Dennis's invitation? Consider some of the answers she might have given, and note the view that Dennis took of each outcome:

"Yes, I'd love to," she replies. Dennis, pleased with his success, quietly offers a sigh of relief.

"Gee, I'd really love to, but I've made other plans. Maybe some other time." Dennis, sorry she didn't say "yes," is still sort of encouraged by her opening remark.

"No," she hesitates. "I really can't, but thanks anyway." This is clearly a setback for Dennis.

(4) *Attribution.* This refers to the reason one finds to explain the outcome that has occurred. On the one hand, you may attribute success or failure to some characteristic of yourself (intelligence, ability, looks, age, personality), or to some aspect of your behavior in the situation (such as amount of effort or tactic used). Alternatively, you may attribute the outcome to something external to yourself, such as luck or fate, characteristics of the situation (the difficulty of the task, the weather, failing

equipment, etc.) or the influence of another person, organization, or institution. An individual generally chooses his attributions in a way which lends support to his initial expectation.

If a person has an expectation of success, even when he sees himself as having failed in a particular instance, he can maintain his positive self-concept and expectation of subsequent success. He can do this by either attributing the failure to some aspect of his behavior that he can change (like amount of effort or strategy) or to some external factor that may be different next time (like the other person's mood). Or he may write it off as a one-in-a-million occurrence.

After thinking about this issue, we happened to be watching the Dick Cavett Show. The championship chess match between Bobby Fisher and Boris Spassky was going to take place within a few months and Cavett asked his guest, Fisher, what it would do to his ego if he lost. To the audience's amusement and our delight, the confident Fisher replied, "I would consider it a fluke."

Taking a positive view of the outcome (as in stage 3) or making attributions that maintain a positive self-concept is not equivalent to rationalizing or lying to oneself. The person who takes a positive view is not ignorant of the negative alternatives. He simply knows that in many cases the positive alternatives are just as likely to be true and that by taking this approach to the situation he maximizes his payoffs.

Oddly enough, though, people are inclined to believe negative outcomes and alternatives are somehow more truthful. Even the most confident people will occasionally have "secret" fears of inadequacy and feel that they are faking it.

© 1972 United Feature Syndicate, Inc.

A failure might be seen as providing a glimpse of the "real you." On the other hand, a person with no confidence who experiences a success rarely believes he has found his true self.

By and large, the person who has a positive self-concept can find reasons for a failure that allow him to continue to pursue his goal with the same motivation, and perhaps with new information to help him. He may even view the setback as challenging. The same person experiencing success takes it as a confirmation of his expectation and feels confident of success in subsequent situations.

When Dennis hears that Marcia is eager to dine with him, he attributes it to the effort he made in combination with his winning personality and youthful charm.

While Dennis is less pleased to encounter "Gee, I'd love to but I've made other plans. Maybe some other time," he chooses to believe that she would indeed at least like to, but honestly had a prior engagement. Consequently, his expectation of eventual success has not much changed. His subsequent reactions to her remain friendly and after a few days he asks her out again.

"No, I really can't but thanks anyway" sounds pretty final to Dennis. However, one "No" does not a failure make. Dennis decides to attribute the rejection to something he can change, like the particular strategy he used (maybe I asked her too late in the week, maybe I asked her too abruptly, or maybe I gave her the impression that all I talk about is work). While not wishing to make a pest of himself, Dennis accepts the setback as a challenge and prepares to set a new plan into action. His persistence may pay off, even if Marcia initially had no intention of embarking on a romantic relationship with Dennis. By spending more time with him she is more likely to recognize his assets and overcome initial hesitations. Ultimately, even if she does reject him, since he is basically sure of himself, he is likely to attribute the rejection to something that is not devastating to his self-esteem. "She thinks I'm too old for her," "Maybe she's inhibited by the fact that I have a daughter her own age," "She may have a rule about not getting involved with anyone at work," "An attractive girl like that probably has a boyfriend already," "I wonder if she thinks that I couldn't take a girl her age seriously and that I just wanted to play around."

Remember, he has no way of being sure what her real intentions were. He can choose to focus on those that will make him miserable, or just as easily he can focus on alternatives that are not unpleasant for him. One is just as apt to be correct as the other, but one approach leads to far less grief.

## The Vicious Circle of Failure

Unfortunately, unlike Dennis, many of us have come to see ourselves in a negative light, and we act in ways that will perpetuate this view. Consider how a person with a negative self-concept, set for failure, would proceed through the four stages.

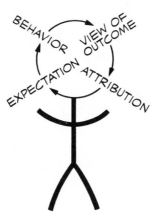

(1) *Expectation.* An individual sets a goal for himself but he is fairly certain that he won't be successful in reaching it.

Unaware of Dennis's encounters, David, a forty-four year old widower, is also considering having an affair with Marcia. However, David does not have much hope for success. In fact, he's fairly convinced that she'll refuse him without giving it a second thought.

**(2) Behavior in the Situation.** Individuals with negative expectations often avoid these situations entirely. However, when they do approach them, their efforts to reach the goal are likely to be halfhearted. They think, "Why waste time and energy, when I'm bound to fail and make a fool of myself." Of course, this attitude does not lead one speedily along the road to success.

> David is tempted to continue admiring Marcia from a distance in order to prevent the possibility of being refused. However, he finally feels that he has to find out one way or the other so he decides to get it over with. The next day he walks up to Marcia and says, "If you're not doing anything else, would you like to have dinner with me tonight?"

**(3) View of the Outcome.** It may seem hard to believe that a person would seek to confirm his expectation of failure. Yet being correct is sometimes more important than being successful. Moreover, when you expect something to happen it takes fewer supporting cues for you to conclude "I knew it," and many more contradictory cues to conclude "I guess I was wrong." The person who is set to fail is more attuned to aspects of the situation that signal failure.

> Assume, as we did before, that Marcia responded to the invitation in one of three ways and note David's assessment of the outcome.
>
> "Yes, I'd love to," she replies. David is surprised, but pleased.
>
> "Gee, I'd love to, but I've made other plans. Maybe some other time." David thinks, "Looks like I was right."
>
> Since David viewed the last statement as a "final" answer to his question, it would have made little difference if she had said "No, I really can't but thanks anyway," even though this reply conveys greater finality.

(4) *Attribution.* A person's negative viewpoint can be even further buttressed by the reasons he finds to explain this failure. If he attributes the failure to something about himself that he thinks cannot be changed (like his intelligence, ability, looks, personality), he is likely to throw in the towel then and there. Similarly, if he attributes the failure to something outside of himself that he thinks won't change (like his luck, or the attitude or policy of others), he is again likely to give up.

Thus, while the positive set led the individual to view difficult circumstances as surmountable, the negative set led the individual to take the view that "that's the way things are (or I am)." While the positive person saw failure as a fluke to be acknowledged and dealt with, the negative person saw it as the typical pattern for himself. While the former was able to maintain his positive self-concept *despite* failure, the latter maintained his poor self-concept *because* of failure. Although "objectively" the same external events (Marcia's replies) might have taken place in both instances, the positive person is ready to give it another try. The negative person, meanwhile, has resigned himself to his fate, resenting himself and/or the world for what has happened.

Even when the person with the negative set succeeds, he does not view it as an accomplishment and does not change his self-image. Just as the positive person views failure as a fluke, the negative person views success as a fluke ("I just happened to be in the right place at the right time"), or as a result of another person's attitude or actions ("The teacher passed me because he was in a good mood"). He can thus maintain the view that without these external circumstances, he would have failed as usual.

It is not that the person with high regard for himself has more guts or can take a beating and come back for more. He just doesn't see things in this way—every setback is not a blow to his ego, does not lead him to question his abilities, does not tell him he will fail in the future. It is precisely because of this attitude that he is more likely to take "risks" and try out long shots. His view of his self-worth is not on the line. The person with the negative self-concept is more likely to stick to "sure things"—failure is painful; it is endowed with all kinds of self-condemning meaning—the risk is not worth it. But succeeding in sure things is not terribly rewarding. That is, in a way, ironic, since the negatively set person will not engage in those behaviors which might allow him to change his opinions about himself. When he does take risks, he usually does it in such a way as to bring about the expected losses.

When Marcia tells David that she'd be delighted to go to dinner, he attributes it to factors that minimize the success: "Because of my position in the company, she might have felt compelled to accept." "Maybe she just didn't want to hurt my feelings." "It could be that she'd go out with anybody." "Who would refuse a free meal?" "She probably just wants to get ahead in the company."

Any refusal, no matter how encouragingly stated, would have led David to admit defeat and to make at least one of the following attributions: "She thinks I'm an old lecher." "She finds me unattractive." "She probably considers me a fool for having asked her in the first place." "A lot of guys my age go out with young girls; there must be something wrong with me." "I have and always will have rotten luck with women." "She probably thinks she's too good for me. She seems so cool and confident—she's probably turned off by how uptight and insecure I am."

### BEAUTY IS IN THE EYE OF THE BEHOLDER

The following true story was the first time one of us realized how important a positive self-image was. Prior to this time I believed that thinking positively would help, but that if you were a loser, walking around telling everyone that you were a winner was pure lunacy. (It was almost forgivable for me to use such expressions since I had not yet studied psychology.)

I was living out in San Francisco at the time. While coming home from work one day I got involved in an accident and required the attention of a doctor. A friend of mine mentioned the accident to his friend, an eager, but not yet established, young lawyer. The lawyer contacted me, and then proceeded to persuade me that I had a case and that he was the one to handle it.

That was the way I met Hank. The impression I got of him after talking over the phone for the next week or so was that he was enthusiastic, good humored, and sort of charming. When he came over to my house to discuss the case further, I had to add unattractive to the list of adjectives.

After we concluded our discussion of business matters, we got involved in a friendly and rather personal conversation. Hank had recently come to San Francisco from New York. He was divorced and was eager to tell me about the marvelous changes in his life. It seemed that his ex-wife had constantly told him how ugly he was. I thought that that was both cruel and accurate—but kept the latter thought to myself. Hank explained how inhibited this made him with other people. "I had little confidence in myself and was enormously shy." I said I couldn't believe that he was ever shy. He recounted some experiences he had had at parties and with clients to convince me. He was successful in gaining my sympathy.

Then he told me how different he was now. He had traveled across the country with the thought that he just might not be as homely looking as she said—so he took some risks. He met many women—some were accepting, and some were rejecting. He gradually improved his opinion of himself. He put this a little differently though: "I slowly started to recognize how wrong she was. Now I know I'm good looking. When I walk into a room people take notice of me and believe it or not (I didn't) the girls are all over me at parties." We talked some more, and then a horn started honking outside. He said it was his new girlfriend picking him up. We went over to the terrace to see if it were she —it was, and she was simply beautiful. For a moment I couldn't believe the whole episode. What was even more bewildering was that I started finding him attractive.

Although Hank's somewhat dramatic tale is not unique, most

people with negative self-concepts never bother to test out other hypotheses about themselves, as he did. While at first he accepted his wife's opinion as indisputable truth, he later formulated an alternative positive view, "I am *not* ugly," and set out to confirm it. Now Hank tells people how to respond to him. His new manner has an air of confidence, and the subtle and not so subtle cues are effective. It is not surprising that most people listen.

Below is the story of Lucy. Lucy has not yet broken out of the vicious circle of self-defeat. She too tells people how to treat her.

### Why Love Lucy?

Lucy is an exotic looking, bright, young woman, both generous and fun to be with. Upon meeting her, men find Lucy extremely attractive. Stan was one such man. He quickly became adoring and was all too eager to put her on a pedestal. Unfortunately, Lucy did not share his high opinion of her and had difficulty accepting the respect he accorded her. Initially Stan assumed that Lucy was just being modest. She'd answer his compliments —"You know you're beautiful," "I think you're great," etc.— with a statement like "You're *just* saying that." Stan, however, never questioned her to find out just what she thought his motives actually were. That was what he'd say if he were *just* being nice, but that was also the way he felt—why didn't she assume he was being sincere?

Lucy feared that Stan, like all the others, would soon find out what a horrible, selfish, shallow person she really was. With each date her worries increased. Finally to alleviate this anxiety and hasten what she thought was the inevitable, she began to inform Stan of what she believed to be the reality. Little by little she tried to dispel each of his "misconceptions" about her. She did this in both action and word. Now when he'd say, "I think you're great," she'd answer with some self-defacing remark like, "If you knew me better, you'd never say that. I'm usually very selfish and demanding." Then to make her point she'd go into action. If he did some minor thing like arriving a little late for a date, dropping ashes on her rug, or not calling when he said he would, she'd start picking on him, and after putting him through her nagging routine, she'd say, "See, I warned you I'm not as nice as you thought." Lucy continued to tear herself down and build Stan up. From this superior position, Stan began to re-evaluate their entire relationship. He became less attentive, less considerate, and gradually less adoring.

Lucy is finally taken down off the pedestal. She is unsatisfied and miserable, and even worse, she thinks she has more evidence confirming what she thought of herself all along.

This vicious circle is repeated with each new man that she meets.

On a few occasions Lucy met men like Greg, who persisted in their adoration despite the evidence she presented to the contrary. In order for this to make sense to her, she had to conclude that they were foolish and indiscriminate, and that her time would be better spent elsewhere.

Lucy's pigeonholing of men has gotten her into a double-lose situation. She wants men like Stan whom she considers percep-tive because they don't want her, and she doesn't want men like Greg whom she feels have poor taste because they do want her.

How can she get out of this bind? Lucy, like many others, will have difficulty improving her self-portrait as long as she con-tinues to commit the *Sin of Nonspecificity*. This is the use of vague generalities to describe your problems—"I'm horrible," "I'm nervous (selfish or inconsiderate)," to name a few possi-bilities. A statement of this kind is difficult to disprove, because it doesn't tell you what particular behavior led to this conclu-sion. Nor does it suggest a way out. What does one do in order to avoid being horrible?

Labelling oneself "horrible" is not only uninformative, it may also be quite damaging. It seems to imply an underlying trait—a basic characteristic that cannot be changed. At best it implies that it may only be removed with major personality sur-gery. Yet when a person examines the *specific* instances that led up to the adoption of the label, he often sees how, without much effort, circumstances could have been different. If he then adopts the new mode of behavior, he no longer merits the label (if indeed he ever did).

If Lucy asked herself: "Why am I a horrible person?" she might say, "Because I make people miserable." While this would lead her to a somewhat better understanding of what she might do so as not to be "horrible," it is still not specific enough. She might then ask: "How do I make people miserable?" and she might answer, "I nag and criticize them." This would lead her to query:

*Q:* Whom did I criticize? When? Why? How?

*A:* Two weeks ago I was picking on Stan for not calling when he said he would. I started yelling "Why haven't you called?" before he got a "Hello" out.

*Q:* Was it warranted? Did he provoke it?

*A:* Yes, he knew I'd be upset if he didn't call.

*Q:* From Stan's point of view would he have thought he had provoked it?

*A:* No, he was probably sure that I knew he'd call eventually (or that he had some good reason for the delay).

*Q:* How might I have stated my concern so that it wouldn't have been received as harsh, unjust or challenging?

*A:* I wish you had called earlier; I was worried. I wish you had tried to call earlier; I was starting to let myself get annoyed. Hi, is everything all right? I thought when you hadn't called earlier something might have happened to you, or perhaps you were angry at me.

The impression we are left with is that all of these last "feeling" statements would be responded to with something like "I'm sorry" followed by an explanation. On the other hand, her original "demand" statement ("Why didn't you call?"—implying he *should* have called) was more than likely to have been met with resentment.

She originally interpreted his not calling in a manner consistent with her self-concept—negatively: He didn't call because he didn't care; He didn't call because my feelings don't concern him; He didn't call because our date isn't as important as his work. And the argument that ensued further confirmed her suspicions.

Instead, she might have considered the possibilities: Maybe he had some trouble with his car; Maybe he wasn't near a phone and taking time to find one would have made him even later; Maybe he didn't have the time and thought I'd be understanding enough to understand; Maybe he had a problem on his mind and just forgot; Maybe he did try and my line was busy.

By attending to any of these alternative explanations, her attitude towards him would not be hostile or defensive. This would in turn lead her to respond differently to him and him to respond pleasantly to her.

Along with this change, it is important for Lucy to look for an alternative positive description of herself. This too will act as a stimulus for a new range of behavior. The positive consequences of this behavior will reinforce the new approach and thereby help to maintain it. To put this another way, with the positive alternatives in mind she will behave differently, good things will happen, and she'll be more likely to continue acting in this way.

We're not telling her to pretend to think highly of herself while she secretly thinks "this is not the real me." The technique will work only if she acts with confidence while she *open-mindedly* tests the hypothesis "this *is* the real me."

This test is more easily made when there is a shift of attention from "all" that she did wrong to the "few" things she did right. The assignment then becomes one of going through all the situations she can remember that she uses to support her negative impression. Taking the situations one at a time, the next step for her is to try thinking up as many alternative ways to explain the specific incidents as she can. Again the more alternatives she can think of, the less likely the one negative alternative she had previously chosen will seem. With practice Lucy should begin the search for alternatives as soon as the incident occurs, thereby avoiding the consequences of negative thinking she previously suffered.

While at first she may encounter some difficulty, after a time she will probably become quite adept at finding alternatives. Since most people have been trained to end their search after finding one "answer," it takes a creative, and even more important, a determined person, to continue the search successfully.

Lucy's self-concept, though extremely negative, was somewhat stable. She had identified certain qualities that she believed she had, and thought of herself in terms of them. When she finally realizes the flaws in her reasoning and the control she has over the specific behaviors she dislikes, she may begin attending to her assets and begin to confirm her positive self-definition. Soon this self-concept will become relatively stable.

The following case of Roger falls into a different category. His self-concept does not rest on his assessment of his own qualities. It rests on his assessment of the qualities of those around him. And as the people around him change, so too does his self-definition.

## Rebel Without a Cause

Roger is a successful insurance broker. His intelligence and wit have earned him the respect of most of the members of his field. As well as being competent in his work, Roger has always been very attractive to women. Yet for Roger, a somewhat angry young man, these qualities do not add up to a stable image of himself. Instead, he constantly compares himself to others. If he comes out on top he is smug—for the moment—until a new threat comes along, someone whom he sees as a little bit better than himself. In other words, every person he meets is in some sense a competitor. When he meets someone, he asks himself:

"Is he smarter than I am?" "Is he more handsome?" "Is he a better lover?" "Is he a better insurance broker?" If—heaven forbid—he believes any of these to be true, he lives in fear and hatred of this person until, finally, he uncovers a crucial flaw.

Besides making Roger's self-concept unstable, this attitude has other serious consequences—it warps his view of other people. If he feels belittled by others' strong points, he will attend to their weaknesses. If he hates others for their strengths, he will seek to prove that they are indeed inferior, either by watching them with an eagle eye set to find faults, or perhaps by forcing them into a losing situation. Since he is something of a male chauvinist, his task is made easier—he can dismiss half of the population as competition from the start. Roger has constructed his world so that he can emerge a winner only when a "self-made" or "Roger-made" loser is nearby.

Roger has also gotten himself into a double bind. He can't enjoy being with people because those whom he'd most like to be with are threatening and those whom he feels most comfortable with, he finds boring. However, he needs people in order to live with himself, to prove to himself that he's not really that bad.

However, Roger *can* change his negative attitudes and begin to form a more stable self-concept. First he can ask himself: "Why am I so threatened by other people?" "Why do the thoughts 'he may be smarter than I am' or 'he may be better looking than I am' make me so anxious?" The reason for his extreme reactions to these statements may lie in the illogical or exaggerated conclusions he draws from them. He may not be aware of the "blow-up" process, but it goes something like this: "If he is smarter, then I am not smart. Therefore he will be a success and I won't." "If he is wittier, then I am not witty. Therefore people will like and admire him and not me."

Implicit in this shaky argument are several contradictory assumptions—people can be ranked with respect to each other on all qualities (e.g., John is more charming than Peter); positive qualities are all or nothing (e.g., if I can't be the best, then

47

what's the use); only the best will succeed (other people will reject me if I'm not the best).

Since most qualities do not have absolute standards, it is foolish to try to rank order everyone on each quality. What is attractive to me may be wishy-washy to you. What is witty to me may be crude or corny to you. By "smart" we might mean interpersonally sophisticated or good in business, while you might mean good in math.

Neither are they all or nothing. Three thousand independent observers may agree that you are more attractive than I, but that does not mean I am unattractive. You may score higher than I do on every conceivable measure of intelligence, but that does not mean that I am not intelligent.

No wonder Roger's self-concept is shaky considering the ridiculously high criterion he has set for himself. "I must be better than everybody at everything." One piece of evidence to the contrary is enough to explode this and tell him he is worth nothing. This is where he gets the idea of "Why bother if I can't be best?" or "Other people will reject me if I'm not best." In the back of his mind is the thought that no one would want to associate with a nothing.

Many people, like Roger, make themselves miserable by dwelling on their liabilities or on things or characteristics that they don't possess ("I am not perfect or infallible"; "I do not have long straight hair"; "I am not very wealthy"); on areas in which they do not excel ("I have no head for figures"; "I sing like a frog"); or on the things they did not attain in the past ("I did not get into Yale"). Focuses like these make self-esteem impossible to attain.

Nobody, not even "the man who has everything," has everything. He too may dwell on his liabilities, but it is just as easy and infinitely more rewarding to concentrate on assets: "I may not have a head for figures, but I do have remarkable social skills (or vice versa), and that's what's important to me."

But before Roger can base his self-concept on his own assets, he must take stock of them. Unfortunately his assessment of his good points is also obstructed by the perfection issue. If he asked himself, "Roger, are you smart?" he might answer "Yes, I guess so," but he'd think "Once I got a D in English, and my college boards were pretty bad." "Are you attractive?" "I suppose," but later he'd think "Several girls have refused me in the past." "Are you a good insurance broker?" "I make lots of money at it," while later he'd ruminate over the cases he messed up.

To this we must ask: How much evidence is enough? How many confirmations of an asset do you require before you are secure and stop harping on past mishaps? Why does Roger need to have scored highest in everything to think "Yes, I'm smart," to have won the heart of every woman to feel, "Yes, I'm attractive," and to have clinched every case to believe, "Yes, I'm a great insurance man"? He has done well in enough things for him to stop punishing himself and, by consequence, all those around him.

When Roger was cocky, angry, and belligerent, it was not difficult to understand why few were inclined to lavish praise upon him or to cultivate a friendship. They, of course, felt that since he was so sure of himself he did not need their compliments. They also felt that if he were going to try to make them feel inferior, they could live without his company. Needless to say, Roger was angry and resentful at the world for denying him the rewards he wanted.

Once Roger has a pretty good idea of his own merits, he can start appreciating other people's qualities without being threatened: "Charles is really bright; maybe he will have some ideas to offer on the new project." "Ed is very clever; I really enjoy his company." "Hal is unusually handsome; I wonder if he'll introduce me to some of his women friends." After Roger forms a positive picture of himself he will begin behaving positively toward others. They, in turn, will start giving him rewards in ways they had not previously done.

In Lucy and Roger we have examined two typical examples of self-induced misery. These vignettes serve to demonstrate how a negative view of yourself may blind you to your own potential.

Many of us are simply variations on these classical themes with different occupations, different physical descriptions, and different unflattering labels. There are probably few who couldn't profit from adoping their new patterns of behavior.

## The One Face of Eve: Narrow Self-Definition

There is another kind of view people often take of themselves that, while not exactly negative, may have damaging effects; that is, defining yourself in terms of only one of the many roles you play.

In all she did, Jane defined herself as Don's wife. When meeting people, she introduced herself as Don's wife. She saw herself as managing Don's house, buying only the clothes Don liked, and cooking basically for Don. Instead of making any personal decisions herself, she left them to him. Although she seemed happy in this role, what would have happened if Don decided one day to pack his bags and leave? Would she find any meaning left in her life? Would she be able to function as an independent person?

Yet Jane filled many other roles while she was Don's wife— she was Greta and Sam's daughter, Betty's sister, Maggie's closest friend, a teacher at Newton High School, a lover of the arts, etc. If she defined herself in terms of all of these roles that she actually performed or some subset of them, then what would happen to Jane if the role as Don's wife were eliminated? While we are not playing down the importance of her marriage, it appears to us that Jane would, in this latter case, consider her life still worthwhile.

Clair thought of herself first and foremost as Harold's mother. No sacrifice was too great—she didn't pursue her career so she could always be home for Harold; she didn't buy clothes so she could give Harold extra spending money. She catered to all of Harold's creature comforts with great care.

Clair's narrow self-definition, in all probability had harmful effects on her relationship with Harold (or on Harold himself). For instance, she probably continued to treat Harold like a baby long after he had left the crib. She might have overemphasized his dependence upon her long after he was ready to assume independence. She might have resorted to guilt tactics when he showered his attention elsewhere. Or she might have sheltered Harold to the point where he did not learn to relate to peers. Aside from the danger of hurting the very object she is trying to protect, what happens to Clair when Harold finally decides to leave home? She becomes a nonentity in her own eyes.

Joel was an all-star bowler. As a boy he worked in a bowling alley setting pins in order to be near the big-league bowlers. At closing time, instead of locking up, he would stay around and bowl a few games—hoping someday his scores would equal those of the greats. At the age of sixteen he became the youngest professional bowler to tour the country and come out tops in the major competitions.

He remained at the top for the next twelve years. His enthusiasm for the sport showed no signs of waning. When he wasn't in bowling matches, he was practicing. When he wasn't practicing, he was talking about it. When he wasn't talking about it, he was thinking about it.

Then, at the height of his acclaim, Joel developed arthritis. Not knowing what to do with himself, he initially refused to take his doctor's advice and give up bowling. As the pain got worse, he had little choice.

But while Joel was busy making a name for himself in the world of bowling, he was also filling the roles of husband, son, father, friend, sports' critic, to name a few.

Jane, Clair and Joel all defined their lives in terms of one person or thing, even though their days were filled with many important people and activities. Under the circumstances, their loss (while usually painful) was *devastating*.

There are several ways in which each of them might have protected himself against the tragic effects of the loss. One is by recognizing the importance of the other roles they played and other talents they had, so that they might fall back upon them. Another is by specifically developing other pursuits that would make them interesting and self-sufficient apart from any one person or thing.

We all depend on other people to some extent and many of us have professions to which we devote much of our time and effort, but when we allow one person or pursuit to dominate our definition of ourselves to the exclusion of all else, we run the same kind of risks as the people discussed here. Since definitions, or labels, lead to behavior, those of us that are broadly defined or "well-rounded" are the best protected against loss of person, limb, or job. The remaining definitions will dictate what to do the day after the rain has stopped.

## Measure for Pleasure: Social Comparison

"Gary, do you want to play tennis this afternoon? Are you any good?"

"As a matter of fact, Bill, I'm pretty inferior," Gary said with a tinge of misery in his voice.

"Let's play anyway, Gary, it'll give us a chance to sweat off some of this fat."

Later that afternoon on the court, Bill discovers that Gary is quite a good match for him. Puzzled by the inconsistency, Bill asked "When you said you were inferior, did you mean to Pancho González or to Freddy, that awkward kid from Yonkers?"

Often we cause ourselves unnecessary grief and feelings of inferiority by bemoaning the fact that we aren't like certain other people. Comparing ourselves exclusively to these people only serves to make us feel worse.

Sometimes the remedy does not consist of either changing ourselves into the something we're not or of giving up the idea of ever being competent. It may simply be a matter of changing our reference group. That is, comparing ourselves to a more appropriate set of people.

We are not suggesting that instead of trying to improve your skills, you should derive superiority by always associating with those who are less skillful than you. We are not suggesting that instead of examining your beliefs, you should always seek out people who will support them and shun those who don't. We *are* suggesting that you be both realistic and wise in your choice of a comparison.

If you are a beginner, compare yourself to a beginner, not to a gold medal winner, or even an intermediate. If you are starting a diet, don't compare yourself to Catherine Deneuve or Robert Redford after the first week, feel utterly dejected, and dash to the refrigerator. (That's why a group like Weight Watchers may be useful. There you are accorded well-deserved praise for reasonable weight loss according to standards tailored to you personally). When joining a new firm, are you going to be depressed because you feel inferior to someone who appears to know all of the ins and outs of the business, or are you going to look to see if the ten years he's been there may account for the difference? However, when your confidence is not on the line, these "champions" may, of course, be used as models.

If you really believe in the "new morality," don't choose a group of friends who will make you feel immoral for practicing it. If you hold certain religious or political beliefs, don't surround yourself with those who will make you feel that there is something wrong with you for holding such beliefs. In short, if you are an outcast in one pond, swim to another. The choice is often yours to make, and the exercise is healthy.

As we discussed in the introduction, marital status may be blamed for one's unhappiness. While neither state (being married or single) is inherently superior to the other, you may feel that the greener grass is on the other side.

Todd is recently divorced. He lives in the same apartment as he did when he was married. All his friends are married and are living the kind of life Todd is most acquainted with. He still does many of the things he did when he was married, but now he does them alone or with his married friends. Going to their homes for dinner or joining them at the movies just doesn't please him the way it used to, since everything he does reminds him of his ex-wife. He is lonely and miserable. The only solution he can see is to find another woman to join him in doing what he's doing. Then he won't have to feel "inferior" and out of place for not being married. An alternative solution would be for Todd to find a new reference group—other single men and women. With them, the conversations, interests, things he wants to do, and things he has to do will be more in tune with present interests. This is not to say that he should stop associating with his married friends entirely, but by defining a new reference group for himself he will alleviate some of the frustrations he encountered before and will be able to see them and the married state in a more detached, realistic way.*

However, choosing an alternative reference group is difficult for the person who is unaware that one exists. Such an individual may feel that he is abnormal for having the beliefs or desires that he has.

Take, for example, the woman who has been imbued from childhood with ideas about the bliss of wifedom and the joys of motherhood. She may experience tremendous guilt when she finds herself unfulfilled by her housework or occasionally resentful of her children. She may feel that this is a personal flaw to be squelched or concealed, rather than a common problem to be

---

* Another aid to reducing his unhappiness would be to change his environment. If he cannot afford to move, he can rearrange the furniture in his apartment and make as many other physical changes as possible. This new environment will have no unpleasant memories associated with it and will therefore not act as a subtle but constant reminder of the past. He may change his hair style and clothes to help him start his new life. While these things may appear to be superficial, they were conditioned to the past, and, as such, they may act as stimuli for memories and behaviors that are best left to the past.

dealt with. Perhaps one of the greatest services the Women's Liberation Movement has performed was to show these women that they were neither crazy nor evil for finding motherhood a chore, washing dishes distasteful, or staying in the house a bore. By pointing out that vast numbers of women shared these feelings, the movement created a new reference group, besides sighs of relief heard 'round the world.

Difficulties like finding the appropriate reference group may arise when people do not share information with each other or when they share insufficient information (only the joys). As long as you are a functioning individual you can be sure that there are other people somewhere who think, feel, or act just the way you do—perhaps many more than you suspect. If you are brave enough to disclose your discomforts and uncertainties to your friends, you will probably find these disclosures met with "phew-filled" statements like, "You must be kidding. I thought *I* was the only one who . . ."

# FOUR

# *Friendly Persuasion*

## PRESENTING INFORMATION EFFECTIVELY

"That was a fantastic lecture. The guy was great. He's absolutely right— it's a crime to put young people in prison just for smoking grass. I sure hope Congress listens to him."

"I don't believe it. I just don't believe it."

"What are you so steamed up about, Barry?"

"What am I so steamed up about! Dad, you're a real hypocrite. I've been telling you the same thing for years, and for years you've been threatening to turn me into the police if I ever tried the stuff. Mom, tell him."

"You know he's right, Bernie."

Bernie is embarrassed. He feels like a fool. He can't quite explain why he was never persuaded before to what he now sees as the only rational position.

Perhaps we can advance some hypotheses. Barry may have

been too emotional so that Bernie never really heard the substance of the message. He may have tuned his son out because he seemed to say the same thing over and over again. Barry's persuasiveness may have been weakened because of his personal investment in the argument's outcome. Or perhaps he precluded a change in his father's attitude by the way he phrased his arguments.

Such high-pitched, ineffective arguing is no stranger to any of us. But why is it so common? Possibly because people give nearly all of their attention to the merit of their argument and fail to consider how those contents are packaged.

But to say that Barry did something wrong in his efforts to win Bernie over is to explain only half of the picture. The lecturer must have done something right. Good speakers, like good lawyers, teachers, or salesmen, are concerned with more than just making valid points. They take great care to create certain sets in the audience, to anticipate their reactions and build upon them, to lead them inevitably to their conclusions.

These people are successful because they realize that there are many possible reactions one may have to any single idea. Therefore, they know how important it is to work out a strategy which ensures that the listener will come away with the very reaction they intended.

Should effective persuasion be their domain entirely? Or are the techniques they practice simple enough to be learned and practiced by everybody?

Before answering this, however, the question that must be answered is: Should everyone want to use these strategies? Some would argue that these techniques can be employed only at the expense of spontaneity. They might insist that if you stop to calculate the reactions to your statements you are more like a computer than a person. But we question the widespread belief that spontaneity is always good. It sounds as though it should always be good. But can't you think of instances where words have spilled out, and your only wish was that you could put them back? People very often hurt each other "without thinking." This thing calling spontaneity is also responsible for a good many misunderstandings—the message received is often very different from the one you thought you sent. Moreover, it often takes more time and trouble to undo the damage you've caused than it would have taken to prevent it in the first place. Hindsight is nice, *but foresight is better*. Thus, if the choice is between spontaneity and effective communication, shouldn't you opt for the latter?

Spontaneity need not be sacrificed permanently. As with most things, after some practice these techniques can become second nature to you. Consider the strain you felt when you first learned to drive. Each operation you carried out behind the wheel required your utmost attention and concentration. But once the skill was well learned, there was an automatic shift to a more relaxed state. Now, while you drive, you are probably able to do such things as carry on conversations and listen to the radio.

For those of you who think this all still sounds too manipulative, we refer you to the opening pages of Chapter 2 where we explained that whether manipulation is viewed as positive or negative depends on the context it is in. We invite you to put the techniques we will describe into the context you deem proper. For those of you who have reread Chapter 2 and are still skeptical, we invite you to read the following pages not to enhance your own persuasiveness, but rather to understand others who are already following the rules we present.

Some people will simply say that while there is nothing terribly wrong with explicit planning, it's just too much trouble. However, when the consequences are important, this is really no excuse. The time spent in aimless worrying is no less trouble and is far less fruitful than structured planning.

By now it should be clear that the purpose of this chapter is to offer guidelines for effective communication. How do you tell somebody something you think they'll hate you for? In our discussion of directed thinking, we will present some hints for organizing the information you now have. We will suggest how you can use this information to put across difficult messages in a way that maximizes the listener's understanding and acceptance. Next, we will demonstrate a variety of useful techniques of persuasion. How do you prevent a person from yelling "sour grapes" when you express dislike for something you can't attain? How can you make sure successful persuasion will endure in the face of contradictory reports?

Finally, we examine what is probably the most widely used but least effective persuasive tactic—the argument. When, why, and how is it used? What purposes does it serve?

## Directed Thinking

"Oh, why did I say that?" "How could I have been so stupid?" If people thought more before they spoke, they'd tend to kick themselves less afterwards. But many people who *do* think before acting still end up black and blue. What do they think about? "Should I say it or shouldn't I?" "I hope she says yes." "What if everything goes wrong?" "What will he think of me?" "I hope I can get up the nerve to ask."

The prevention of those unsightly bruises, however, lies not in thinking per se, but rather in directed thinking. By *directed thinking* we mean clear specification of what you hope to achieve and systematic consideration of all those factors which will influence your achieving it.

### MAY THE BEST MAN WIN

Hal is in a bind. He knows that within the next month one of the company's sales representatives will be promoted to regional manager. He thinks he has a fairly good chance of getting the position. The problem is that Catherine, Hal's boss, has asked him to go to Illinois to close a contract with an important client. Realizing the importance of the assignment, he didn't know how to say no. Unfortunately, he had already promised his friend Glen that he would be best man at his wedding. The two events coincide. Hal is in the position of having to refuse his boss or back out on his friend.

Hal decides that an obligation to a friend comes before personal ambition. Besides, he made that commitment first. But he is still plagued by the thought that this action will cost him the promotion. How can he bring himself to tell his boss that he had no right to accept the assignment? "I'll tell her I can't go because I just found out that I have to have an operation. No, I might not complain about the right pains. Maybe I should tell her that a relative died and I have to stay here to make all the funeral arrangements. Does that sound too much like an excuse? I can't lie. I know whatever I think up I won't be able to pull off. Besides, I'll feel better being honest. I'll just tell her the truth. I'll go into her office and tell her I decided not to go."

For days he can think of nothing else but the mess he is in. He waits until the last possible moment to perform this odious task. Finally, the day arrives. He walks into Catherine's office and delivers his rehearsed statement: "I'm sorry I didn't tell you this sooner, but I won't be able to go to Illinois. I promised a friend that I would go to his wedding."

While Catherine says she understands, she is still somewhat annoyed that he agreed in the first place and then waited so long to let her know. She is left with the impression that Hal is irresponsible. This is just what he was afraid of.

There is no *one right way* to handle any particular situation. However, some approaches are much more likely to be successful than others.

Hal's approach may have seemed rational and appropriate to you. We are not suggesting that it wasn't. It might have turned out fine. Catherine could have filled in the pieces of information Hal left out—but she didn't. He could have insured Catherine's understanding of his position by considering a number of factors he ignored.

One of the most important of these is arriving at a clearly defined goal: What is it that you'd like to achieve? It would seem from Hal's statement to Catherine that his goal was to inform her of his choice. If this were truly all he was interested in accomplishing, then by any standards, be succeeded. It appears to us, however, that Hal was hoping for more than that. He was hoping that Catherine would accept his choice and respect him, or at least not think less of him, for having made it. He didn't want Catherine to think he was irresponsible or uninterested in his work. On the other hand, he did want her to think that although he cared very much about his work, he had certain obligations to keep and could therefore make no other choice. Clearly then, Hal should have included these considerations in his goal.

Concretely defined goals serve to direct your thinking. They answer the question: "*What* do I want to achieve?" Directed thinking leads to direct solutions. Thus the next question becomes: "*How* am I going to achieve this?"

In answering this question, there is an overwhelming amount of potentially relevant information available. In fact, there is so much information surrounding each situation you may encounter, that it is humanly impossible to use all of it. "She's in a good mood in the afternoon. Peter backed out on her yesterday. Is my tie pressed? She told me to speak slowly. It's raining out. Her father was a quitter. We don't get along well when the vice president criticizes her. She's most receptive to me when we're alone. The coffee lounge is conducive to friendly conversations," etc.

Considering that this is only a minute fraction of the information available, it is no wonder that people feel overwhelmed. There is, however, a viable alternative to throwing your hands up in frustration, muttering "I can't be bothered with all that," and using virtually none of the cues at your disposal.

The alternative is to formulate meaningful questions that may be used to select and organize the information. Without this organization, the information is chaotic and unmanageable. The questions provide a *systematic* way to take account of a good deal of information without being overwhelmed.

*Q*: **What do I know about this other person, his relationship with me, and the present situation which might be helpful?**

(1) How has he or she reacted to similar situations in the past with me and with others? What approaches worked and which didn't?

In thinking over Catherine's past behavior, Hal realizes that she gets furious when told what to do. He recalls that she enjoys thinking of herself as generous and self-sacrificing. Most people in the office know that Catherine resents being "treated like a lady" or flirted with when it comes to business matters. Hal also remembers a few instances in which Catherine's authority was questioned. There was the time when Leonard went over her head and asked the vice president for a raise, and Kevin refused one of her assignments. It wasn't that long ago that Bruce's wife was going to have a baby, and he announced he was taking an extra week off from work. She blew her cool in each case and started to exercise her power arbitrarily.

(2) What is the person's impression of me? How might this action create or reinforce negative impressions?

Catherine thinks Hal is bright and good at his work, but she often jokes about his being somewhat of a Romeo. Hal's decision to attend the wedding might make her feel that he's irresponsible and that he cares too much about social matters. She once remarked that the most important test of an employee is the way he stands up under pressure. She might think he is taking the easy way out because he doesn't feel up to handling this important deal.

(3) How does the person feel about the topics of concern?

Hal may ask himself whether Catherine is sentimental about personal matters, like weddings, or whether she views them as commitments to be fulfilled. He remembers the many times she's complained about attending social functions given by friends and relatives. Bored as she knew she would be, she would grin and bear it because of the obligation she felt to them. Hal also knows Catherine takes work seriously and won't accept less from others.

(4) What other factors are unique to this person and may be relevant to the situation?

Hal knows that Catherine tends to be grouchy in the morning. In fact, almost all of their disagreements have occurred before her second cup of coffee. He remembers that a board meeting is scheduled for this week. After one of those she'll be in no mood for his news.

In summary, Hal knows that Catherine doesn't like not being consulted or being told what to do. He knows that if the situation is not handled properly, she might think that he is irresponsible or weak or that he places his social life before his work. He knows that fulfilling obligations is important to her. In addition, he knows that Catherine is moody in the morning and hassled after board meetings.

**Q: Taking this information into account, what is the most effective way of communicating your decision?**

Hal may now fit these pieces together and arrive at a plan of action. If there are just too many pieces, he may single out the most important ones and formulate an approach around them. However, he should certainly check back to make sure that the approach is consistent with the information he hasn't incorporated.

Rather than announcing his final decision as he did before, Hal decides to present his dilemma to Catherine. One afternoon he knocks on the door of her office and after some preliminary conversation he brings up the trip to Illinois. He tells her that he has a problem and that he hopes she'll understand. He continues by saying that he agreed to go to Illinois because he knew how important it was to the company, although he had already promised his friend that he'd be the best man at his wedding on January 2. Only later did he fully realize that it wasn't right of him to break his prior commitment. He emphasizes what a difficult choice it was for him to make. To show her that he considered her in his decision, he tells her how aware he is of the inconvenience he might have caused her. After a pause for her reply, he suggests that perhaps the trip could be delayed a day or two so that he can still handle the deal, thus further stressing his concern for his work.

In this way, Hal has led Catherine through the stages of his decision process, so that she will then, hopefully, reach the same conclusions. In doing so, he has shown his respect for her authority and has given her the opportunity to be both generous and compassionate.

It is important to realize that acting in a manner which will influence the other person favorably is not tantamount to lying or being superficial. It is simply a matter of emphasizing those factors which will eliminate misunderstanding and preserve the relationship.

Of course, there are never any guarantees. No matter how much information you take into account, there is always the chance that some extraneous factor you didn't consider (or didn't even know about) will be influential. However, by considering the questions discussed above, you substantially increase the likelihood of successfully persuading the other person of your position.

Although we have presented these suggestions in an occupational setting, we are by no means limiting their applicability. Consider how you might make use of these ideas if you found yourself in the situations described below. To remember the questions to ask yourself, keep in mind these variables: the other person, your relationship with that person, and the situation.

(1) A daughter trying to persuade her mother to let her go away for the weekend. (A girl who knows her mother is somewhat "old-fashioned" and is afraid of gossip may do well to use

a different approach from a girl whose mother is "trying to be with it." And clearly, both girls would be wise to consider their mother's opinions of such things as where the happening is going to take place, what she likes and dislikes about the male in question, etc.)

(2) Mother trying to convince daughter not to go away for the weekend. (The mother who knows her daughter is impressionable and flighty is dealing with a different situation from the mother whose daughter is mature and clear thinking. Their approaches should reflect this difference.)

(3) One friend trying to persuade another to lend him his new car for a few days. (Should he emphasize their friendship, the care he'll take of the car, or perhaps the urgency of his need?)

(4) A student trying to persuade his teacher not to give an exam. (Should he stress that the exam is unnecessary because he "knows" they all know the material already, or because the idea of exams is degrading and contrary to the spirit of the course?)

By directing your thinking to the information you have about that other person, your relationship with that person, and the situation, you are in the position to put this information to use and thereby be more persuasive.

Directed thinking allows you to systematically exert your control over important situations. It also has another beneficial consequence. The very knowledge that you have control over a situation should serve to eliminate much of the anxiety regarding its outcome. That is, when the outcome is viewed as out of your hands, a lot of aimless worrying takes place; when it is viewed as being within your sphere of influence, you tend to be more relaxed and act more confidently. Moreover, the fact that your attention is devoted to formulating your plan of action means that it is not devoted to futile worrying.

When we do not have much information, educated guesses are in order. With the knowledge of a person's age, socioeconomic status, profession, sex, we can fill in the missing data with the information we have about others who share these characteristics. These guesses are, of course, based on stereotypes, and as such are often inaccurate. But any information is better than none.

> Elliot has just transferred to a different college and has to persuade the Dean to give him credit for course work taken at his previous school. He thinks, "most deans are favorably disposed to serious students, so I'll take my books with me into his office. Since he's probably in his forties or fifties, he's likely to be less radical than I am, so I'll start with the traditional courses I took and leave the classes in sensitivity training and civil disobedience for last," etc.

Even when we have virtually no information at our disposal, we are far from powerless. There are many useful techniques that can still be employed. Below are examples of several strategies for successful persuasion.

## *Direct Disclaimer*

People are often unaware of how the context in which statements are made may influence the thinking of their audience. They believe it is solely the message that is persuading them one way or the other. Before he was "put on the spot" by his wife, this is exactly what Bernie thought. If his wife hadn't pointed out that his son did say many of the same things the Congressman said about marijuana, this is probably how he'd continue to think.

Bernie's son was unpersuasive, in part, for the same reason that a lawyer arguing against No Fault Insurance would be. What do the two have in common? Each appears to have something to gain by arguing the particular side of the argument he has chosen. Their apparent gain clouds the merit of their position. Shrugging his shoulders, the listener thinks "What else would you expect him to say?" The implication is that the speaker is hiding some important facts favoring his opposition. Contrast this with the case of a lawyer advocating the use of marijuana and a teenager arguing against No Fault Insurance. After leaving these discussions, the listener is more apt to be contemplating the merits of the speeches than the motives of the speakers.

But what if the lawyer honestly felt that the state's adoption of No Fault Insurance would be harmful to the public—does he have to keep his opinions on the matter to himself? Of course not. But can he be persuasive?

To enhance his chances of inducing attitude change, he has an effective strategy at his disposal. He can disclaim the notion that he is arguing the side he has chosen because of his personal gain. Naturally, this is necessary only when the audience is forewarned about the position to be taken or is likely to put two and two together fairly quickly. In this case, the audience knows he's a lawyer and therefore expects him to argue against No Fault.

The disclaimer consists of stating that what the audience expects to hear because of your bias, is true in spite of it.

> "Of course, you'd expect me to be against No Fault Insurance. But if we can put that aside for the moment, I honestly believe that you'll be sorry if it's adopted . . ."

By opening your remarks with a disclaimer you may tame a relatively hostile audience. Prior to your communication, they may think they can see right through you: "A lawyer arguing against No Fault Insurance! What does he think I am, an idiot?" But by putting yourself in their hands, you may succeed in disarming them.

Moreover, because you have expressed an understanding of how the listeners feel, you have, in their eyes, increased the similarity between yourself and them.

Here are just a few of the many instances in which disclaimers may come in handy:

(1) You've just received a notice of merit (praise from your boss, on "A" on a difficult exam, an athletic trophy) and want

to share the good news with friends. There's no need to deny yourself this pleasure because you're afraid they'll think you're conceited. Statements like "I know this may sound pompous, but a really nice thing happened to me today . . . ," "I know this is boasting, but . . . ," or the like are apt to leave the listener happy for you rather than resentful.

(2) You want to state an unpopular position in a discussion with conservative friends. If you come right out with it, they won't listen to the rest of your argument. Adding a disclaimer will serve to lower their resistance. "You probably think being against marriage is another lunatic, radical idea, but it's not as crazy as it sounds . . ."

(3) How about the case in which a teacher has to present some rather dry material to his class? Rather than just going on

*"On your mark, get set—now I hope this doesn't sound too bossy—GO!"*

with the presentation, hoping they stay with him, he may include a remark like "I know this may be boring, but hang on a few more minutes because it's essential for understanding what's to come." The students are likely to leave the classroom feeling a lot more satisfied than they would have without that warning.

Before using a disclaimer, however, it is important to estimate how likely it is that your audience is actually thinking about what you plan to disclaim. If the odds are that they are thinking nothing of the kind, then you run the risk of putting ideas in their heads—that is, of making them question what they wouldn't have questioned otherwise. Imagine that an aspiring suitor, eager to please his new girlfriend, brings wine, flowers, or some small gift with him on many of his visits. She is delighted by his thoughtfulness and attention. Then, on one of his visits, he casually remarks, "I hope you don't think I'm trying to buy your affection." While the thought had never entered her mind, it is now not likely to leave.

Another example of an inappropriate disclaimer can be seen in the following situation.

> The setting is a small real estate agency where the employees are all rather friendly and informal with each other. On this particular day, one of the senior agents is extremely busy but has a client arriving shortly. Thinking that one of the younger agents may have some time to spare, he asks him to do him a favor and show the client some property. "Excuse me, Dan, would you do me a favor . . . I don't mean to pull rank on you . . ." Dan, to be sure, would have been glad to do it, but somehow bringing rank into the picture has taken the pleasure out of it.

The disclaimer can work for you or against you. Careful judgment on your part will determine the direction.

### Indirect Disclaimer

Consider the following situations: a person makes a negative evaluation of his ex-spouse; a student failing a course wants to have it eliminated from the curriculum because he thinks it's both outmoded and a waste of time; a young 5′ 2″ female who weighs 190 pounds is speaking against mini-skirts because she thinks they are in poor taste. Being on the receiving end of these communications would probably leave you pointing a finger and silently yelling "Sour grapes."

It is, of course, entirely possible that these people have reasons to back up their beliefs that have nothing to do with what seems obvious. In fact, in the first two instances, it is even likely that these beliefs were causes of the outcomes rather than rationalizations of the outcomes. That is, the spouse may have wanted the divorce because he thought his wife was selfish and cold, and was not speaking ill of her out of bitterness. As for the student, if he thought the course was a waste of his time, he would probably have had little motivation to study. While there is no analogous explanation for the young lady, it is quite plausible to believe that she is really against short skirts and would continue to be so even if she were 70 pounds lighter.

There are always several alternative reasons why a person may be for or against any particular person, place, or thing. However, if their personal involvement is very apparent, it will make one explanation most salient. In our examples, divorce, a failing grade, and excess weight are the attributed motives that cloud the other possibilities.

Since their remarks are so "obviously" face-saving, it is improbable that a direct disclaimer would dispel this notion. Picture someone stating with a straight face: "I'm not saying this out of spite, but my ex-wife . . ." or "I known you'll think I'm saying this because I'm failing, but . . ." or "It's not because I can't wear them. . . ." Even with the disclaimer, the listener will think that the speaker is trying to kid himself.

A totally one-sided account, especially when negative, leads the listener to suspect an ulterior motive, even when he has no evidence for this. When an ulterior motive is apparent, even though untrue, your credibility is reduced to an all time low. To make matters worse, you look foolish in the process.

71

To lend more weight to their assertions, an indirect disclaimer may be useful where a direct one would fail. An indirect disclaimer consists of providing a more balanced account of the person or thing you are evaluating. That is, if you are trying to show a side you think is realistically negative, it is to your advantage to mention some positives as well: "My ex-wife is intelligent and charming, but also somewhat selfish and cold." "The course is well organized and well taught, but it is utterly irrelevant." "I think short clothes are fine for beaches and recreation, but they're inappropriate in places of business." These statements, unlike the others, do not lead the listener to infer that your judgment has been clouded by your emotional investment in the issue.

## Initial Agreement

In his younger years, Russell worked as a door-to-door magazine salesman to help put himself through school. Needless to say, his memories of the job provide him with countless stories for relatives and friends. He recently recalled a situation where he pulled off what his boss thought was an amazing feat.

As you may know, many apartment buildings and private houses have relatively inconspicuous signs warning solicitors to keep away. Most salesmen obey. Russell usually did also. However, he remembered the time that he passed this rather ordinary house with a rather extraordinary "No Trespassers" sign on it. It was so big that he remembered it as having covered nearly a quarter of the facade!

While much amused, he took this as a challenge to his salesmanship. He rang the front bell and when the lady of the house came to the door he went into his presentation. He told her that he couldn't help but notice the sign. He continued to say that he thought she must have had some awful experiences with solicitors to lead her to deface her home in that way. He said he could understand just the way she felt, since so many of them are brash and inconsiderate. She then recalled some tales of woe.

72

He told her that he, too, was selling magazines and even though he thought he was offering a good deal, he wouldn't think of telling her about it unless she insisted. She did. He did. She did.

What was it about Russell's presentation that got him the sale? Although we can't be sure, he did use some researched techniques that probably contributed to his success. One of these is *initial agreement*. Letting a person know you agree with him from the very start is effective even if you later contradict yourself. This is because it ensures that your message will be heard. But more than that, it favorably disposes the person to both you and your statements.

By virtue of his initial agreement, Russell labels himself as a "similar other." Once our lady of the house identifies with him, at least to some degree, it becomes difficult for her to later reject anything he may say. Most people, unfortunately, dichotomize the world into good and bad. Russell is initially defined as good, and the belief is that good people don't do bad things.

We are not judging Russell's morals. We are merely reporting how he maximized his chances. Perhaps the deal was indeed a good one. Then she may be fortunate that he presented it in such a way as to give her the opportunity to examine its merits.

Imagine, for a moment, that Russell was trying to persuade some teenagers not to use heroin. If he presented himself as a member of the "establishment," a "dissimilar other," and argued the unpopular position from the start, he would probably end up talking to himself.

As with all means of persuasion, the ends may or may not justify them.

## Inoculation

Traditionally, the approach taken with soldiers training for combat has been to instill them with the ideals of their country as armament against the cruel and unusual punishment they might face in the hands of the enemy. They were expected to be loyal to these ideals and to divulge nothing more than their name, rank, and serial number. If, however, they had been forewarned about the kinds of arguments the opposition would advance in their efforts to obtain information, they might have shown even greater resistance to this influence. Those who knew what arguments to expect (such as false information about who was winning the war or when it would be over), and, most important, those who were given information to *counter* the claims the enemy might make, were the best prepared. If the practice of giving soldiers information to counter the claims of the enemy were a matter of routine, as the research suggests it should be, the soldiers would be able to withstand an incredible amount of psychological pressure. By knowing what some of the opposition's arguments were likely to be, they would be equipped to refute them when and if they were presented.

How does the prison camp illustration relate to your everyday life? The analogy may be useful to you in two ways—to you as a communicator and to you as a listener.

On occasion, you will be giving information that is likely to be refuted by someone else at a later time. When this is probable and you are eager to prevent a change in their attitudes, it might be wise to inoculate your audience. Build their resistance to counter arguments by informing them of what the opposition may say and then refute those claims.

You and your lover are splitting up and you're feeling great bitterness. It's important to you that your mutual friends come over to your side. To accomplish this, you describe your ex as an incurable disease and recount all of those heinous things he (or she) did to plague you. No doubt you are now the possessor of all their sympathies, so you can calm down. However, your friends will be confused and hard-pressed for an answer when the "enemy" finally gets in touch with them. Your points will be weakened as they listen to the other side of the story.

Of course, the most successful way to preserve your dignity and friendship in a situation like this is to speak highly of your opponent—but most people find this much too difficult. If you must indulge, then for your own sake at least inoculate your audience against the conflicting version they may hear in the future.

Imagine that you are the parent of two children. Your older son comes and tells you that his brother broke his toy. You're likely to believe him until the younger is confronted with the crime. The two boys start arguing over who the culprit is. Of course, you have no way of knowing at this point. However, imagine how much more certain you would have been if your older son had reported the incident and told you his brother was going to deny it for fear of being punished.

Suppose as a listener you don't want your mind changed because you think there would be harmful side effects. What do you do to resist attempts at persuasion? Just as you can inoculate other people, so too can you inoculate yourself. You can think up or seek out counterarguments before you are bombarded.

Thus, as a communicator or as a listener, forewarned is forearmed.

Direct and indirect disclaimer, initial agreement, and inoculation are techniques arrived at by observations of interpersonal situations and substantiated by experimental research. These examples we've presented by no means exhaust the possibilities. You may arrive at some of your own in a similar way. Experiment—see which approaches are best received and try them out in new situations.

The strategies suggest different ways of presenting information; they do not require distortion or deception. It is the responsible individual who uses them wisely. And it is the wise individual who is aware of the dangers of their irresponsible use.

### In the Heat of the Fight: Arguments

Arguing is another persuasion technique. It differs from the other strategies we've talked about both in its subtlety and its effectiveness.

It is a widespread belief that arguments are necessary. Anyone who seeks a serious relationship free of battles is considered naive. There are also a few psychotherapists who assert that arguments are healthy. Their therapeutic sessions consist of teaching the unhappy couple the "right" way to fight. Don't be misled into thinking that we feel this kind of fighting is necessarily destructive to the relationship. Nor do we think that if all arguments were eliminated you and your partner would automatically be happier.

Arguments are generally regarded as a means of resolving conflicts. The participants "actively" try to persuade each other to change their opinions. While it is doubtful that they serve this function effectively, they do serve additional purposes.

Research has shown that people will work to maintain an optimal level of arousal, stimulation, or environmental variability. When there is too much arousal, people work to reduce it. When there is too little, they will work to increase it. The latter may be conceptualized as a fight against boredom.

Therefore, if a person is bored, arguments may provide increased stimulation or introduce variability into the relationship. On the other hand, if a person is overaroused, as when he is angry, he may argue to let off steam.

While arguments, viewed in this way, may serve a useful purpose, two additional questions arise: (1) Do they serve the purpose of resolving the conflict? (2) Do they have undesirable side effects?

Do arguments serve to resolve conflicts? In a word, seldom!

When an argument begins, the point of disagreement is usually clear. However, the evidence you present to convince the other person (and resolve the conflict) gets more and more muddled as the argument progresses. In the heat of the dispute, where the level of emotion and noise is high, it is difficult to organize and present your views coherently. Yet in your eagerness to hammer your points home, you blurt out these ill-considered thoughts. Moreover, the urgency of having your say, prevents you from listening to your "opponent."

Quite naturally, the other person who is going through the same thing is not listening to you either. It is difficult to be persuasive when there is no audience.

What happens when all the evidence is presented and the argument is as heated as ever? You start to say the same things over and over again. To make your point more compelling, since it didn't get through the last time, you increase the volume with each repetition. The interchange begins to resemble a shouting match, with each contestant trying to preempt the other. Then, pressed for new evidence, you usually succumb to the "blitz" strategy. That is, hit him with all you've got! You dredge up every bit of information from the past, no matter how tangentially related, and throw it into the arena. Much of this evidence is damaging and insulting, and any valid point gets lost in the barrage.

By now, winning is more important than resolving the conflict. The goal becomes "crushing your opponent's ego." Suppose the other member has realized his error—at this point it is impossible for him to admit it. If he does, he looks foolish for having argued it so violently for so long. So the argument continues until fatigue sets in.

While the point of disagreement might have been clear and relatively minor at the outset, it is no longer so. Differences multiply as new issues are dragged in and hurled back and forth. An argument over a wrong turn on the parkway might now include mothers-in-law, moustaches, overweight, and infidelities. Even when the two sides are really converging, the psychological distance between the arguers has become so great that you feel you differ more than ever.

Do arguments have undesirable side effects? It is not difficult to see how a clash of such intensity can have further repercussions.

Issues which were dragged into the argument that were not sources of conflict in the past may become so in the future. What if you discover in the course of an argument that the other person finds your habits infuriating, hates your best friend,

or thinks you're too fat? You may become defensive about these issues or resentful of the other person for having flung them at you in such a callous way. They may now provide fuel for future fights or depressions.

What if during an argument, in order to "keep the lead," *you* gave into this temptation to hit below the belt? You no doubt hurt your partner more than you ever intended. On days when there is no argument, but he's plagued by self-doubt, he may recall those words to himself as supporting evidence. And *if* he lets you in on his thoughts, you'll have a tough time convincing him that you only said it to get back at him—that you said it because you were angry rather than because it was true.

What about the other function that arguments may serve—that is, to change your level of arousal, to keep you from being bored, and to tone you down when you're hyper? Consider the fact that both people might not be at the same level of arousal to begin with. If you're bored and your partner comes home exhausted, it is thoughtless to impose an argument on him because you need a change. Similarly, if your partner is content, but you need to let off steam, it's selfish to scorch him in the process.

Even if we put aside the issue of being considerate, arguments, used in this way, may prevent you from finding more constructive ways of coping with your problems. They may keep you from asking important questions: Do I need other interests? Do I need to find other ways to relax? Is there a better way to solve our disagreements?

## I'd Rather Fight Than Switch: Illegitimate Anger

On many occasions people illegitimately lash out at others. When the person who caused the frustration is different from the person who subsequently bears the brunt of it, this illegitimate action is called scapegoating, or displacement. A country taking out its ills on some minority group, or a person yelling at the family after getting reprimanded at work, represent classic examples.

Of the two, the second illustration is more likely to hit home. In most cases like these at least one person usually realizes that the aggression was displaced. Even if only after an argument, they realize that the little incident which set the argument off could not alone explain the anger that was vented. Oftentimes the apology will be accompanied by statements like "I had a hard day at the office," "I was really annoyed at your friend," "I was worried about the exam," etc.

There is, however, another kind of illegitimate lashing out where the cause is much more subtle but the result no less volatile. What is worse is that here the wrong person usually ends up taking the blame (if blame is ever justified) and making the apology. Before we explain this more fully, examine the following situation and see if you can pick out what's wrong.

This couple has seen better days together. In an attempt to rejuvenate the relationship, the wife decides to surprise her husband. She is going to prepare all his favorite foods for a romantic feast. After returning from the supermarket loaded down with heavy bundles, the preparation begins. Clams casino, prime ribs and chocolate soufflé were just part of the menu. The entire day was spent cooking and baking the gourmet delights. She had it down to a science. All would be ready at precisely six o'clock, the time he most enjoyed eating dinner. At 5:45 the telephone rings. It's her husband. He called to say that he still has work to do and won't be able to leave the office for another half hour. While the dinner wasn't exactly ruined, the tastes did not reflect the hours of preparation. By the time he got home, she was furious. Her argument seemed sound—he should have called her earlier. His only defense was the loud retort "Do you think I was playing all day!"

Since she had extended the greater effort, and in his behalf as well, she was declared the winner.

Compare this to the following interaction between the same couple four months earlier.

Things are running behind schedule at the doctor's. The wife is being kept later than she had anticipated. She won't get home until after 5:30, so she'll have to throw something quick together for dinner. At 5:45, the telephone rings. It's her husband. He called to say that he still has work to do and won't be able to leave the office for another half hour. She now catches her breath and stops running around the kitchen. When he comes home they have a normal dinner.

Since the husband had done the same thing on the two occasions, the difference in the wife's reaction was a function of what *she* did and what happened to *her*. His intention was not more negative nor his action more inconsiderate in one case than the other. In this sense, her reaction was "self-induced." We can sympathize with her in the first situation. It must have been frustrating for her to go to all that effort only to have it fall flat. However, her lashing out at her husband was not justified. She thought she was yelling at him because he "caused" such inconvenience, yet how was he to know what was going on in his kitchen miles away.

To illustrate the point further, consider another example. Son tells father he needs the car Saturday in order to pick up some things at a friend's house. After the father informs him that he has a golf game on Saturday, the son offers to drop him off at the course and be back to pick him up after the game. The father reluctantly concedes. Saturday rolls around, he delivers his father as planned, and drives off. Not as planned, the father's golf partner doesn't show up. He's not terribly disappointed because he has a lot to do at home. But how is he going to get there? When the son finally arrives, he gets blasted.

People don't always blow up in situations like these, but they almost always feel resentful ("I made him a beautiful dinner and *he* didn't come home"; "I lent him the car and *he* left me stranded here"). By failing to identify the cause of their anger or frustration, they use their time to get more and more furious at the other person. If they thought about how much their *own* situation and their *own* feelings were contributing to their anger, they might use the time to calm down.

### ARGUMENTS AS AVOIDANCE

The Harrisons' dinner is tonight and Charles is dreading it. His stomach gets tied in knots every time he thinks of pandering to all those hypocritical in-laws. They'll grill me about my work and then won't listen to my answer. They'll ask embarrassing questions at a deafening volume. I'll have to mouth things I don't believe and go along with their inane statements so Alice won't get upset. As the adrenaline pours into his system, the dinner takes on the proportions of a nightmare.

When Charles and Alice get home from work, she asks him to

help her put some groceries away. He complies, grudgingly. He starts complaining that they've been spending too much money on food lately. "What's eating you?" Alice asks.

Charles: "Lay off, huh?"

Alice: "I don't like the way you're acting."

Charles: "What are you, some princess?"

And so on.

Charles storms out, yelling to Alice that she can go to the dinner herself. He won't be caught dead with that pack of phonies.

He has provided himself with a convenient out. Now that they are in the midst of a quarrel, Alice won't expect him to go to dinner.

Instead of skirting the issue as he did originally, some may say that Charles should have just told her outright that he didn't feel like going. But when he has tried this in the past, Alice would answer sternly by saying "We have to go," and then the fight ensued:

Charles: "I don't have to do anything."

Alice: "It's just not right. Don't you have any consideration?"

Charles: "Yes, I considered it very carefully."

Alice: "You never want to see my family. . . ."

And so on.

Charles didn't feel like going through that again.

If a fight didn't take place, Alice would start pleading with him. "Please go as a favor to me." But Charles feels that he's done this particular favor too many times already. Moreover, by making statements like these Alice unwittingly offers tacit agreement that it *will* be awful for him. A more effective strategy would be for Alice to direct his thinking to those aspects of the situation that are not unpleasant for him. Uncle Zeke, the lawyer, will be there, so we can get advice on what to do about that accident. Dad just got a copy of that book you're interested in and said you could borrow it. The food is usually great, etc.

Besides, another point Charles should realize is that it is probably within his power to exert some control over the topics of conversation at dinner. He can steer clear of topics where he feels he'll have to mouth things he doesn't believe or where he knows he'll be annoyed by the views expressed, before those conversations get underway.

While the saga of Charles and Alice leaves us with the impression that Charles was a culprit for behaving so immaturely, the picture can't be as one-sided as it appears. There must be something Alice could have done to alleviate the situation.

She might have prevented the whole issue had she acted differently from the beginning. When the invitation was extended, Alice no doubt accepted first and then informed Charles that they were going. No matter how pleasantly she put it to him, he felt he was forced into it. People tenaciously hold on to what they perceive as their freedom of choice. Any attempt to usurp this freedom is reacted to vehemently. To avoid this, Alice could have given Charles the opportunity to make the decision to accept:

> Alice: "My parents invited us for dinner next week. Would you like me to tell them no?"

She has given Charles a choice—even though it is a choice between being a bastard or a sport. He chooses the latter:

> Charles: "No, I guess we have to go."

Both are happier with the decision.

While this illustration makes a number of points, the main thrust of it is that arguments are often used as a means of avoiding things people don't want to do but feel they have to. Start an argument over "X" and you won't be expected to do "Y." This devious mechanism may close the door to understanding in a number of situations. Take the bedroom as another example. It is anticipated that your amorous lover will make an advance. You're not in the mood but don't know how to say so. To avoid the issue, you strike first by picking a fight during the eleven o'clock news. True, you're no longer "expected" to make love, but isn't that hitting below the belt?

It's never too late to open a closed relationship. In some of our other examples, we've stressed the importance of anticipating the other person's reaction to your behavior. This is not the problem here. Each person thought he knew very well how his partner would respond. In fact, that's why he avoided an open discussion. The mistake they did make was in assuming that this was the *only* way the partner *could* respond. Certainly if you persist in behaving (e.g., stating your position or making excuses) in only one way, you should not be surprised when your partner's response is consistent.

Therefore, the recommendation becomes: Take time to consider the alternative ways you can state your case in order to achieve the desired result. This involves understanding why the other person feels as he does and incorporating some of the persuasive techniques we've mentioned to reflect this understanding.

What if, in spite of all we've just said, you still feel that arguing serves some useful purpose? Then we recommend the following rules to help keep the explosions from leaving scars.

(1) When there's doubt, don't leave it out. When your statement implies that you are right beyond a shadow of a doubt (You're wrong; That's nonsense; He's an ass; It was your fault), the other person is likely to perceive this as a challenge. He may meet it by defending himself aggressively or attacking you personally. Here the listener is led to dispute *who* is right, rather than *what* is right. Many arguments can be toned down simply by using a phrase or two to preface the remarks you were planning to make. Phrases like "it seems to me," "I think," and "in

my opinion" lead your disagreeing listener to try to change your mind through persuasion rather than force.

(2) Don't fight equally hard for everything that you want. If you do, you make it difficult for the other person to discriminate what is important to you from what is just said for argument's sake. As an example, the difference between going on a vacation and going out to dinner gets blurred when fireworks accompany both discussions.

People usually assume that when something is important to them, it is important to everyone, or at least its importance is recognized by everyone. Consequently, when an important issue does come up and is not reacted to with extra concern, it may be enough to infuriate you. Next time stop to ask whether you've allowed the person to appreciate its importance.

(3) Don't use the same strategy over and over again. You'll lose your audience before your points are heard. Once the listener can predict just what you are going to say, he will become less attentive. How many times can "You don't care about my feelings" or "You never try to understand my side of it" lead the listener to reconsider his position, before these phrases are met with boredom and disgust?

(4) Be aware of the fact that useful information is rarely communicated in the heat of a fight.

In this chapter we have dealt with ways of giving information so as to be persuasive. Initially we discussed how you can lead another's thinking to favorable considerations by first directing your own thinking. Then several techniques were presented to help further these considerations. Finally, arguments were demonstrated to be an ineffective persuasive strategy.

We have emphasized the fact that valid statements are often discounted or misinterpreted by others because they are not presented effectively. By the same token, reasonable requests are often dismissed or denied for similar reasons. In the next chapter we suggest ways of avoiding these disappointments.

# F I V E

# *Asker Aids*

## MAKING REQUESTS

We have just spoken about ways of directing or changing a person's *attitude* with the goal of getting him to agree with you.

Now we will focus on directing or changing his *behavior* with the goal of getting him to agree to your request.

Of course, attitudes and behavior are not independent. Attitudes are predispositions toward behaving in certain ways. By changing a person's attitude, you may influence his future behavior. So, for example, if you convince a person of the validity of minority rights, he might be more likely to vote for a bill on equal employment opportunities. If Hal was successful in directing Catherine's attitude toward him, he stood a good chance that she would promote him. The reverse is even more apt to occur: by changing a person's behavior, you are very likely to effect a change in his attitudes—simply because people tend to infer their attitudes from their behavior. This change in attitude will occur provided there are no compelling external justifications, like love or money, for the person's changing his behavior.

It's really behavior that you're most concerned with. In campaigning for a cause, it's nice to have persuaded someone that the cause is worthy and should be supported. But that won't help you at all unless he actually digs into his pocket. Observable overt behavior—statements and actions—are public and as such represent commitments.

In Chapter 2, The Politics of Control, we discussed the use of rewards and punishments, as means of controlling behavior. If a person complies, his response is reinforced and is therefore more likely to recur. This may be thought of as a strategy of persuasion. But what if you just asked someone to do you a favor? Would they see the potential rewards for complying? Finding the answer to this question is the task of the present chapter.

Most of the situations we will present here can be analyzed in terms of rewards and punishments and do employ those principles, but we have generally chosen to take a more global approach. We have chosen to concentrate on those factors that *precede* the other person's behavior (his granting or not granting the request) and affect the likelihood that he will comply with your request. We will discuss such variables as phrasing, timing, presentation, and preparation—and show how they can be used to increase your chances of getting help in emergencies—or just urgencies.

In asking a favor, when should you direct attention to your own need, and when should you direct attention to the other person's obligation?

How do you establish yourself as a person who merits the favor you are asking?

When does a person agree to a request that is contrary to his desires although consistent with his beliefs?

How can you virtually guarantee a decision in your favor without appearing to restrict the other person's freedom of choice?

How can you aim your criticism to bring about changes without having it backfire or without wounding the target?

## *How to Succeed in Getting Help Without Really Dying*

Suppose you were ravenously hungry, and you needed to have some papers copied in a hurry. You could ask an acquaintance to do this favor in any number of ways. Examine just two of the possibilities and predict which is more likely to get compliance:

(1) Hi, Would you do me a favor? Would you please xerox these for me? I have to go to lunch.

(2) Hi. I really need this xeroxed in a hurry. Would you do it for me? I have to go to lunch.

At first glance, the two alternatives may seem very similar. The major difference between them is very subtle. It involves the way the listener's attention is directed. In a manner of speaking, the first case directs the listener's attention toward his responsibility to do the favor. It is as though you are asking: Is he the kind of person who does favors for people? The second case directs the listener's attention to your need or plight. If he responds favorably to this request, it will probably be out of sympathy.

Before you answer which of the two phrasings is more likely to get help, it is important to realize that the request made was illegitimate. Going to lunch is usually not an emergency. Therefore, the favor is illegitimate because there's really no reason you couldn't or shouldn't copy the material yourself. Remembering that the first case directs the attention to the listener and the second directs attention to the urgency of *your* need, it should be clear that in this instance, the first example would be more effective.

The first case is called a target-oriented approach because attention is directed to the target of the request, i.e., the potential helper. The second case is referred to as a victim-oriented approach. It directs attention to the victim, i.e., the person in need of help.

The order of the words you speak is also an important variable. Some people make requests ask-backwards. It is the opening statement that characterizes the kind of approach it is. Therefore, if your request is illegitimate, you would not be wise to open with a statement like "I have to go to lunch," for this would direct the helper's attention from the start to the illegitimacy of your need, as opposed to his ability to help you out.

Can you think of the type of situation in which a victim-oriented approach is better? If your need is just, emphasizing that need will pay off. Thus, if your finger was injured so you couldn't work the xerox machine, using a victim-oriented approach like "I hurt my finger. Would you please copy this for me?" is likely to be successful in getting you that helping hand.

Another subtle factor that will affect your likelihood of getting help is the number of people present when the request is made. This is best seen in a somewhat different context. Suppose there is an emergency. The *more* people there are present, the *less* likely you are to get the help you need. This is somewhat counterintuitive. You would think that if there are several people present, at least one would come to your assistance. But research has shown that this just isn't so. You may be more willing to accept this conclusion if you can relate it to your own experience. Perhaps you can recall the many newspaper stories about victims of rapes and murders who cried for help to the crowds of bystanders present but to no avail. The explanation for this phenomenon is that there is a diffusion of responsibility. The more people present, the less responsible any one person feels.

Of course, you can't arrange your emergencies so that there is just one bystander present. Nevertheless, there are a few things you can do to protect yourself. You can increase your chances of getting help through eye contact. A blank stare into a crowd is ineffective. Without any eye contact people feel somewhat deindividuated. That is, they tend to lose their identity. A decrease in identity goes along with a decrease in responsibility. When Ku Klux Klanners hide their identities under sheets or executioners cover their heads, it is much easier for them to carry out their atrocities. In the same vein, it is harder to refuse a favor when the asker is looking you straight in the eye—you are no longer anonymous. Therefore, when you need help, single out someone in that crowd with your eyes, and look directly at him while you make your plea.

In addition, instead of an empty cry for help, make your plea explicit. Although bystanders observing the emergency are unlikely to offer aid, they are rarely apathetic. It is often an emotionally distressing situation for them as well as for you. They are not likely to be clear thinking. Just yelling "Help!" doesn't leave them knowing what they should do. Consequently, they do nothing. Thus, if you were being raped, beaten, or robbed, and you yelled "Get the police," "Hit him over the head," "Stop that thief with the black bag," etc., you would increase your chances for aid. While this has not yet been tested out experimentally, the assumption is: The more specific you make your request, the more likely you are to get compliance.

This should be true for almost all situations, not just emergencies. Consider the request, "Will you help me answer questions three and four on my income tax statement?" vs. "Will you help me fill out my income tax statement?" In the first case, the person knows just what will be required of him; in the second case, he doesn't know what he's letting himself in for.

Thus far we have said that without these devices (eye contact and request specificity), the more people present, the less likely you are to get help. But with them we can begin to see how the presence of many witnesses may work to your advantage. Let's go back for a moment to the situation in which you are asking an acquaintance to xerox some material for you. Imagine asking the same favor when there are observers present. The fact that the response is being witnessed should make a difference. You have directed the plea to her and have asked her to assume the responsibility for fulfilling it. The bystanders now judge whether or not the responsibility is taken.

In the same way, in the emergency situation, if you single out one person and direct your request to him, the rest of the crowd bears witness to whether or not he carries out his responsibility.

## Limited Choice Strategy

When a person is confronted with a limited choice, he will most likely take one of the alternatives offered. Haim Ginott, in *Between Parent and Child,* offers what is now a classic example. He suggests that in teaching a child how to make decisions, he should be offered a limited choice to begin with: "Do you want scrambled or fried eggs for breakfast?" The greater part of the decision has already been made—he is going to have eggs—and the child now deals with the choices which remain. Under these circumstances he is unlikely to respond "Pancakes."

Much the same is operative in the following situations:

Supervisor to employee: "Would you prefer working overtime Thursday or Friday?"

Student to teacher: "I can't take the scheduled exam because I'll be out of town next week. Should I take a make-up or do a paper?"

Husband to wife: "What day next week can my friends come over for a poker game?"

The questions are phrased as though it is a *given* that the event will take place. The respondent is just given some say in when it will take place or what form it will take. In essence, the asker is presenting a multiple-choice question in which "none of the above" is not an alternative. Rarely will the listener go beyond the choices. More rarely will he go back and question the initial assumption.

Contrast this with the husband who asks: "Can we have a poker game here next week?" By virtue of his having asked the question, he has implied that there is some reason why he shouldn't have that game. The wife then begins to think of the reasons for not having it. With those odds, he'll probably never get to see his full house.

The same is true for the student who asks: "Is it all right if I miss the exam?" If there weren't some reason that it wouldn't be all right, then why would he ask? It is rare, for instance, to hear someone asking "May I buy you a small present?" or "Can I brush my teeth?" When the answer is almost unquestionably "yes," then the question need not be asked.

On the other hand, people don't like to be told what to do or told what is going to happen, when it concerns them, without being included in the decision. The employee will resent the supervisor who "orders" him to work overtime on a particular day. The wife may resent her husband if he announces that he is going to have the game at their house next week. Similarly, the teacher will probably be indignant toward the student who declares that he'll have to take a makeup because he'll be out of town for the scheduled exam. The strategy we have presented, then, maximizes your chances for success because it incorporates both of these notions—stating your request as a given and presenting a choice.

There are, however, limits to any strategy. Imagine if someone asked you, "Would you like to go to China or Africa on our vacation?" It is doubtful that you would let the spending of thousands of dollars pass by as a given. Furthermore, if the choices offered are foreign to the listener, it becomes likely that he *will* question them. Similarly, if the event or activity is one which has no precedent in his experience, he may react with bewilderment—"Do you want to do skydiving this weekend or next?"

Barring unusual circumstances like these, if the choices seem appropriate, and the event is a familiar one, this approach is most effective.

How does it feel to be on the receiving end of this strategy?

When a person has unlimited alternatives to choose from, it is much harder for him to make a decision. It is far easier to answer the question, "Do you want to see the movie 'The God-father' or 'Fiddler on the Roof'?" than "What do you want to do tonight?" There are so many choices for the latter question that you may be at a complete loss for an answer. There are so many considerations that it may be difficult to know on what basis you should make the choice. What aspects of the situation should you take into account? In the face of all these candidates, many never come up for nomination, let alone a vote.

It is true that people like to be given a say in matters. Having the freedom of choice gives you power over the situation and this gain in responsibility enhances your self-respect. However, decisions like these are often more of a burden than a booster. People have a penchant for responding to situations in the way that requires the least effort. Therefore, by asking open-ended questions like "What do you want to do tonight?" you are usually forcing them to exert more mental energy than is desirable to them.

Back to you. It is unlikely that, when questioned like this, the listener will scan more than two or three alternatives before stating his choice, a choice which may fit in poorly with your plans. He might answer by saying anything from "Go to sleep early" to "Clean out the office." The likelihood of his coming up with your preference is at a minimum. However, by employing the limited-choice strategy with both parties participating in the decision, the result is more likely to provide mutual satisfaction.

### *Setting the Stage, Act I: Countering Objections in Advance*

There are many instances in which you can set the stage for your request on an earlier occasion. Here your ingenuity really comes into play because there is no clear formula that we can provide. The only guidelines we can offer are: (1) try to predict just what the listener's negative reaction would be if you simply made the request, and (2) try to make the two events (i.e., your advance statement and the request) seem unrelated—that is, be subtle.

A few examples may make this clearer. You want to borrow an electric drill from the shop at work. Your request is likely to be refused because the piece of equipment is expensive. You stop by the shop a day or two prior to asking the favor and in the course of the conversation mention how important it is that people take good care of equipment, or that most people don't realize how precious good tools are (implying that you do). When you finally ask the favor, this information should play a part in his decision.

You want to borrow an electric mixer from a neighbor who hates to lend things because people are lazy about returning them. In a conversation you initiated, you casually mention how irresponsible people irk you. ". . . Why, he said he'd return it a month ago and still hasn't." A few days later you make your request.

Your friend doesn't want you to make that long drive to visit him. He's afraid you'll get into an accident on the way. During your phone calls you subtly build his confidence in your driving by relating stories of your feats behind the wheel. "An idiot looked like he was intentionally trying to run me off the road yesterday, but there was no problem. I didn't realize I had such good reflexes." "Driving at night really isn't uncomfortable for me any more," etc. Remember though—to be effective, these statements, or ones like them, have to appear to have nothing whatsoever to do with your eagerness to drive out to see him.

Think of those situations in the past where you found yourself needing a favor, and where you knew on what grounds you were likely to be refused. This technique probably would have been useful to you then.

### Setting the Stage, Act II: Agreement on a Related Issue

We are more jovial, outgoing, and assertive at some times or with some people than others. By the same token, we adopt many different roles in the course of a day. Thus, there are likely to be many inconsistent images projected. However, this is not the kind of consistency or inconsistency we are interested in talking about. In spite of these moment-to-moment or person-to-person fluctuations, we like to think that we maintain a somewhat stable set of values which guide our actions. Ideally, if we express certain beliefs and values, then we try to make our words and deeds consistent with them. If a person is in favor of abortion, then we expect him to allow his daughter to have one if she wants it. If a person values freedom of speech, he should not object to an extreme right- or left-winger speaking on campus. Failure to follow through on these beliefs may earn one the label "hypocrite."

While consistency is generally seen as something to strive for, we still witness a great deal of inconsistency between people's expressed attitudes and their overt behavior. Why is this so? Why do people often contradict themselves? Sometimes it is just not possible to act in accordance with your beliefs. Take, for example, the person who believes in a cause and is asked to contribute money or time to it. It may be that at the time he is asked he really can't spare either. Extenuating circumstances like these are not the only reasons for inconsistency.

A person may not realize that his actions are contradictory. At one time he may express the view that integration is desirable, and on some other occasion he may speak against minorities moving into his neighborhood. He may argue that marijuana is harmless but later punish his children for using it. If the two events are unconnected in his own mind, then he is unaware that they appear contradictory.

Another reason for inconsistency stems from concern with the immediate situation. When we are interested in winning an argument, making a business deal, or gaining approval, we may focus on the rewards that a certain statement or action will bring. We may get so involved in the present that we respond without concern for how consistent it is with our previously expressed beliefs.

Yet we maintain that if possible and if aware, people will try to appear consistent to a given audience. The greater is their awareness that an action will be seen as hypocritical, the less likely they are to do it.

How does this help you in getting people to agree with your requests? It suggests that if, shortly prior to making a request, you can get the person to make a statement that is consistent with granting your request, you're likely to get compliance.

This is related to our previous discussion of setting the stage for your future request; by taking into account the person's probable reaction to your request, you can offset it in advance. In that instance, it took the form of *your* expressing views which would counteract his objections. In this case, it is a matter of *his* expressing views which will negate his own objections later.

Suppose a wife with a career would like to ask her husband to take some responsibility for household tasks. She knows he considers himself liberal and egalitarian, but also knows that he considers household chores "women's work"—somewhat inconsistent views! She may avoid hearing his objection if, a while before making the request, she invokes his sense of equality: "Don't you think men whose masculinity rests on stereotyped sex roles are pathetic?" Having agreed with this, he will later find it difficult to refuse to help around the house on the grounds that it is women's work.

While we're on the topic, suppose a woman would like to get her company to substitute "Ms." for "Miss" and "Mrs." on the addressograph. If you were she, using the hints provided in the preceding story, how would you go about this?

Since we, too, are egalitarian, let us not leave you with the impression that this is a plan for women's use alone.

Suppose a man who believes that both sexes should be treated equally, is not down on housework in general, but can't stand

97

doing dishes in particular. By using another couple as an example, he starts a conversation with his wife about how important it is that people who are close be willing to help each other. He continues by saying that people also have a responsibility for *choosing* the favors they ask. Since she agrees that it's unfair to ask people to do things they really dislike when they can help you out in other ways, she has no defense when he brings up his hatred of dishes.

Consider another example.

A man would like to get time off from work to attend a professional convention. He knows that the boss likes his employees to be leaders in the field, with fresh, modern approaches. He also knows that his boss often criticizes people for short-sightedness, that is, not making little sacrifices in the present for the sake of future success. However, our man is aware of the fact that his request may be refused on the grounds that the company can't spare him now. Therefore, shortly before making the request he engages his boss in a conversation about how many businessmen become so immersed in day-to-day work that they lose sight of the broader picture. Boss nods his head vigorously as our man goes on. "They fall behind on current practices and don't see what competitors are doing—and it's the company that loses in the long run." Several days later, he goes into the boss and says with a great deal of enthusiasm, "Remember the conversation we had the other day? Well, I have a great chance to put that into practice. . . ."

While you have to make sure that the person sees the connection between the view he has expressed earlier and his answer to your request now (so that one may influence the other), you must take great care that he doesn't feel trapped or tricked. If he does, he may comply this time, but not again. Your future questions may be met with a suspicious "What are you getting at?" Thus, once again, subtlety is of prime importance.

The other person may very well grant your request in order to avoid appearing hypocritical. However, another factor is also working to your advantage. The request may seem quite reasonable to him in light of the views he has recently expressed. His agreement may not be a reluctant, face-saving device at all, but rather a more enthusiastic endorsement of an action that is compatible with his own goals.

In the examples we've presented here, it was very important to the requester to get compliance. There were times, however, when the other person in the interaction really wished he could refuse. Quite naturally, there are occasions on which we would like a person to feel free to refuse if he so desires. At times like these, it would be foolish to structure the situation so as to make it difficult for him to refuse. But if lack of structure is your strategy, be ready to hear a response that may not be to your liking.

## Russell Sage, Rosemary, and Time: Obligating in Advance

Most people meet their obligations. But how do you get someone to obligate himself in the first place? Certain relationships are so structured that the feeling of obligation is already built in. Parents consider certain obligations to their children as part of parenthood. A teacher considers an obligation to his students as part of his tutelage. Doctors consider helping the sick an obligation to themselves and their profession. People consider helping their friends when they need them for important things an obligation of friendship. But such a sense of obligation can hardly be called into play in most everyday situations.

Rosemary has agreed to give a lecture at the Russell Sage Foundation three weeks from Saturday. While she is eager to speak to the group, she does not relish making that drive alone. To remedy the situation she calls a friend. After telling her about it, she asks her if she'd consider accompanying her. She adds that they'd have to leave at about 7 a.m. to get there in time. Her friend considers herself a night person. Consequently, one of the worst things in the world to her is getting up early in the morning. But the trip sounds like fun and it's difficult to imagine how tired you're going to be three weeks from the present, so she commits herself.

Had Rosemary waited until two days before the trip, she would have been less likely to get a commitment. The closer you get to the date, the more likely it is that a friend will have made other plans. However, this is not the only reason. The closer you get to doing the favor, the more salient the negative features of the task become. Thus, with just two days to keep in mind, Rosemary's friend is apt to be focusing not on the positive reasons for going, but on the early hour and the long drive.

It is rare, if not unheard of, that you ever ask someone to do something that is totally positive. Although not necessarily of the same magnitude, for every advantage there is usually a disadvantage for engaging in that behavior. However, the gains and losses become prominent at different points in time. The advantages are clear when the event is to take place some time in the future:

> "Sure I'll take care of your dog while you're away." The person thinks about how affectionate the dog is, how much fun it will be to play with, how excited it will make his nieces when they visit, etc. He's not blind to the discomforts it will cause; he's just not concerned with them now.

The gains are apparent and are fun to think about. However, as the time of the event approaches, the disadvantages gain prominence. The possible losses begin to cause him worry.

> "I'll have to get up earlier every day to walk him. I hope he doesn't ruin the furniture. What if he gets sick?"

Without the prior commitment, he'd be likely to change his mind. But now it's just too difficult to back out. He is obligated to go through with it. But the picture isn't really that bleak. When he begins to meet the commitment, the advantages will usually take precedence once again.

Perhaps if you are married, you can think back to the time you first made the decision. You were no doubt happy and excited, but as the date approached, so too did your fear. Aside from the commitment to each other, if you sent out invitations or told friends and relatives, you made a public commitment. That was the factor that was going to help you keep your word. After the ceremony, you probably breathed a sigh of relief and were glad you went through with it.

Couple this with the fact that most people don't like to refuse to do favors. Then, in a sense, by giving someone the chance to say yes well in advance when the advantages are salient, you are doing them, as well as yourself, a favor.

### I May Be Wrong but I Think You're Wonderful

When you think highly of a person and let him know it, he is both flattered and eager to maintain your favorable impression. Lest he forget, sometimes it is wise to reiterate your high opinion to ensure that he will act in accordance with it.

Since most people are insecure, and insecurity is by definition uncomfortable, people will be glad to accept your praise. While part of each of them will be thinking "you're just saying that," another part will be hoping your statements are true.

When all this information is taken together, it leads us to another plan of action for bringing about change: Praise in advance.

"I called because I know you're the kind of friend who comes through when you need him."

"I'm glad you're not the type of person who gets uptight when . . ."

"I wouldn't tell you this if I didn't think you were big enough to take it . . ."

"You know, you're really a very _____ (generous, considerate, warm, charming, etc.) person."

101

Even if there is doubt in your mind as to whether the person does in fact display the quality in question, an expression of confidence often acts as a self-fulfilling prophecy—he will behave so as to fulfill your expectations of him. He should be more than willing to prove himself worthy of such high regard. If he doesn't, then he can't accept your compliment.

Those who comply because of your use of this approach will be happier for it. Without the use of this strategy, many people still might comply with your request but more begrudgingly or resentfully. With it, they are allowed to feel magnanimous. And why shouldn't people feel good about what they do for others?

## Damned if You Do, Damned if You Don't

Before dinner: "Honey, let's go to that new restaurant for dinner tonight."

Later that night: "You spent too much money. You know we can't afford it."

Earlier: "I stopped off at the bakery on my way home from work and got your favorite eclairs. Here, try one."

Later: "You know you've put on some weight lately. Better watch it."

or

Earlier: "Would you stop off and get my favorite eclairs?"

Later: "You're not helping me with my diet."

Before party: "I really don't feel well. Why don't you go without me? Really, I mean it. I'll be fine."

After party: "You went out and had a good time. I had to stay here alone."

Sometimes it doesn't pay to grant a request. In these examples both parties acted in good faith initially. But one of them is punished for his well-intentioned compliance. He or she is scolded for being a spendthrift, criticized for putting on weight (or blamed for spoiling a diet), or made to feel guilty for going to the party.

If you ask someone to do something and then punish them for it later, they are less likely to do you favors of this kind in the future. How would you feel if you were asked to fix something, for instance, and then were yelled at for scratching it? Or

if a friend asked you to be outgoing with his friends, and then cut you off whenever you began a conversation? Would you be dying to comply on the next occasion?

Hardly.

People who are eager to please become less and less eager as they are subjected to more and more of these exasperating experiences.

This may seem clear to you because you're reading the contradictory messages right after the initial request. However, when some time has passed to separate the two, this clarity is often lost. Consequently, people are often unaware that they are sending double messages until their requests are met with disgust. All that they can be sure of is that the relationship isn't what it once was—"Why, I can remember when you used to love to do things for me!"

Is there a moral? If there is, it must be: Don't contradict later, what you've requested now. This requires that you think the favor through to see if you really want this particular person to do this particular thing on this particular occasion, before asking for it. Otherwise, you're likely to ask the favor and then feel that you *must* contradict yourself. If this becomes the case, you can still eliminate the frustration for the favor-doer and maintain your favor-asking power.

Consider the following two revisions, and see if they meet this goal:

> "I know it was my idea to eat out and I really enjoyed it. But I guess we have to start economizing."

> "Those eclairs were delicious, but I'm going on a diet now, so please help me out by not bringing them home even if I ask you to."

Our general recommendations, then, are:

(1) Acknowledge the fact that you made the initial request.
(2) Thank the person for complying.

(3) State your request in terms of the future (since the damage is already done).

Alternatively, since your comment serves no immediate purpose, perhaps you can save it until the next occasion arises. "Would you do me a favor? Could you fix this. Please be careful not to scratch it because it's very delicate." "Please don't go to the party without me. I really missed you the last time when I stayed here without you."

Of course, it is often very difficult to delay your comment—you may be very upset that a precious item has been marred or really frustrated while you spent the night alone instead of at the party. The first impulse is to relieve this frustration by yelling at the person who appears responsible for the damage. But further thought would tell you that *you* may have been responsible for your own misery and that nothing is gained by this action. It won't correct what's been done, and it's a slap in the face to the person who meant well.

But how do you keep yourself from getting angry?

When you think about the end result (a scratch on a precious vase, your getting fat, his spending too much money, etc.), you feel like exploding. When you attend to the person's intentions, you're grateful. Therefore, if you want to hold yourself in check and reserve your comments for later, the course your thoughts should take is clear.

### Critic's Choice: Criticism

Tom: "That was a pretty stupid thing to do. Can't you do anything right?"

Denise: "I just meant to see if it would fit. I didn't think that it would break."

Tom: "That's right, you didn't think."

Denise (with a tremor in her voice): "Leave me alone, I can't stand you."

Tom: "You know, the trouble with you is that you can't take criticism."

Criticism! Is that what it's called? Hopefully, she won't believe him. If she does, then we might ask, "Is she likely to benefit from his comments?" It's doubtful.

Criticism is often used as an expression of contempt or lack of patience on the part of the critic. As such, it is understandable why people don't react kindly to it.

Let's put this kind of criticism aside for the moment, and look at the case of a critic who is honestly trying to be helpful and would genuinely like the person to change.

How do people usually respond to such criticism? Why? How can the criticism be offered so as to maximize its effect?

What are some reactions, other than gratitude, to well-meant criticism? One is "Who the hell do you think you are?" Suppose that someone you hardly consider a master of the English language began giving you pointers on your speech. The critic is perceived as setting himself up as an authority—without justification. His help is received with anger and indignation.

Often the target of the criticism becomes defensive. He may not question your right to offer criticism, but it may be rejected out of hand as he begins to justify why his way of doing things is the right way. In more extreme cases, the critic might be labelled unreasonable, unsympathetic or unpleasant.

A third undesirable reaction, oddly enough, can occur when the criticism is seen as valid and is accepted. Unfortunately, the person may read more into your remarks than was actually meant. He may see it as a more general failure that he cannot rectify. He may label himself "stupid" or "clumsy" or "born to be fat," thus confirming the incompetence he already felt. The criticism may lead to resignation, rather than an attempt to change.

Oversensitivity to criticism, however, is not entirely *their* problem. Rarely is the criticism being offered constructive in nature. If your interest is in changing another person in some way, rather than letting off steam, constructive criticism is a prime requirement. But for criticism to be constructive, the aspect you want changed must be changeable, and the means for making the change must be obvious. Criticizing someone for having brown eyes or being too short certainly wouldn't qualify under these conditions. How about telling someone they are too poor or not very bright? Although characteristics like these are changeable, and the means to change may even be obvious, in most cases the changes are hardly feasible. Therefore, criticisms of this type would still not be considered constructive.

We even question whether bluntly telling someone they've gained weight is a constructive criticism. How has it been helpful? Since you're usually the first to know if you've added a little extra, you've hardly been given new information. When criticism consists of information you are all too aware of already, it often has the effect of making you depressed or frustrated. And in the case of the person who's put on weight, it usually results in an extra trip to the refrigerator.

Okay, now suppose your criticism *is* constructive. How do you present it so it will motivate change? To some extent, the best strategy to use really depends on the person at whom the criticism is directed.

Most people respond well to praise. Therefore, it is often wise to praise what they have done right before finding fault, or instead of finding fault with what they haven't. In the same way, some people require an expression of confidence to give them the assurance to act on the criticism. Virtually all people appreciate this.

Some people are motivated by failure. For them, just pointing out a deficiency might spur them to overcome it, while for others this tactic might lead to anger or sulking. For them, an unfavorable comparison with another person can lead them to strive for improvement, although it leads others to drop out of the race. Yet even these people who are motivated by failure are sensitive to the *way* failure is presented and are apt to respond more favorably to both you and your criticism if it is given in a *positive* way.

Another point to recall is that the "public faces" people wear often project greater confidence than they actually feel. We may therefore tend to deliver criticism more harshly than we should, believing the person can take it. Maybe he can, but why should he have to?

Therefore we feel that, regardless of the person you are trying to change, the following strategies serve to make the criticism more palatable and are preferable to ungarnished fault-finding.

### COMPLIMENTS FOR CHANGE

Compliments are pleasing to just about everyone, while harsh criticism is almost always a slap in the face. Keeping this in mind, perhaps it is possible to use the former to soften the blow of the latter. Giving any kind of compliment before the criticism should work in this way, but we have something more specific in mind. We are thinking of compliments that are tied very closely in meaning to the critical remark. Thus, if your criticism is about bitten fingernails, the compliment may be about nice hands; if the criticism is about hair, so too may be the compliment, etc. Not only will the blow be softer, but, what is more important, a behavior change may result. At least the person who is the target of the criticism will be emotionally capable of evaluating your remarks, rather than spending his time cooling off or planning an attack.

Let's consider a few cases where one person is eager to change an aspect of another person's appearance or behavior. We'll present a thoughtless, but common, criticism first in each case and then offer what we consider to be an improved version. It is up to you to do the evaluating. It will probably be easier to discriminate between the two if you imagine yourself as the target of the criticism in each case and try different people in the role of the criticizer. Once you can experience the difference as the object of the remark, you should be more willing to change your own critical approach.

A woman just returning from the beauty parlor is met at the door by her husband:

(1) "You don't look very good—your hair is teased. Next time why don't you ask him not to tease it?"

(2) "You look so nice when your hair isn't teased. Why don't you ask him not to tease it next time?"

A lover of good food expresses his appreciation in a rather robust way at dinner parties:

(1) "Do you have to belch so loudly? Can't you imagine what they must think of you?"

(2) "You make such a good impression on people. But I think they may question it when you belch so loudly."

A person shows his advisor the work he has done:

(1) "These few things are not very good."

(2) "I like the project very much, except for these few things."

Along the same lines, it is possible to precede the criticism by a compliment and phrase the criticism in positive terms as well.

"I like the project very much. If you change these few things it'll be even better."

Instead of saying, "Such and such is bad, please make it good," we could say essentially the same thing by stating, "such and such is good, please make it better." People are usually more motivated to make a *good* thing *better* than to make a bad thing good. Although you are talking about the same amount of work in both cases, one is perceived as less work and more worthwhile.

One of the best ways of giving criticism is also the most direct. Ask the other person how they would like you to express your complaints. Then follow their advice. You are bound to win. If they react to your complaints with resentment, then their own advice was ill-conceived—something they are not likely to admit. If they listen to your request, then you've succeeded.

A roommate has the habit of leaving clothes lying around the apartment.

**By December 31:** Pat has tried to reward every neat attempt Ronnie makes, but this method was taking too long.

*January 18:* Pat: "Please don't leave your clothes lying around the apartment."

Ronnie: "Don't tell me what to do."

*January 20:* Pat: "You're usually so helpful, but do you think you could help me by keeping the apartment neat?"

Ronnie: "Don't talk to me like I'm a two-year-old."

*January 24 (4 p.m.):* Pat: "I've tried every way I know how, but I still can't figure out how to ask you to pick up after yourself without you resenting it. How do you want me to ask you?"

Ronnie: "I don't know."

Pat: "I'm serious. Just tell me and I'll do it."

Ronnie: "Just tell me what you want done without getting excited or obviously trying to keep yourself in check."

Pat: "OK."

(*7 p.m.*) Pat: "Please don't leave your clothes lying around."

Ronnie: "All right."

Pat: "Thank you."

## INDIRECT COMPARISON

For the people who read more into your criticism than is intended, you may find it better to give the corrective information in terms of *another* person who makes a similar error.

Message for Michael: *"Don't butter up the boss; everyone else resents it."*

"Mike, have you noticed how Cliff has been playing up to the boss lately? I hope whatever his reason for it is, he cuts it out soon. The guys are starting to resent it."

Message for Betsy: *"Don't be superficial."*

"You see that car over there, Betsy? I bet there's a good chance that the person who owns it can't afford to. Some people think that the better the things they own are, the better they are. Isn't that ridiculous—especially when they don't even earn the money to pay for it? Why do people insist on being so phony?

Message for Joey: *"Don't be so self-centered."*

"I'm not sure why, but I find that guy on T.V. offensive. He reminds me of the kind of person who never stops talking about himself. You know, the type who tells you how they are, but never stop to ask you how you are."

Michael, Betsy, and Joey will probably start making some changes. Since the comments concerned another person, they were able to evaluate the remarks from a distance. Any interfering personal involvement was eliminated. And what is perhaps equally important, they did not lose face in the process.

On the other hand, this technique will be ineffective unless, in the course of your comments on someone else's behavior, the person becomes aware of what *he himself* has been doing and how people are reacting to it.

If he fails to see the connection, then your answer is to opt for one of the more direct approaches—like positively phrasing your criticism or using the method that follows.

## DIFFERENT OR DEVIANT?

If you think you're the only one who is doing a certain thing or thinking a certain thought, you may begin to doubt your own judgment. (This is not the case, of course, when the whole community is praising you for your genius—a rare occurrence!) Generally, people do find safety in numbers (i.e., safety in conforming to the norms of their "group").

It is somewhat perplexing then that people go to great lengths to try to *appear* different. They put a good deal of time and money into wearing clothes that are different from everybody else's, decorating their homes differently, taking up unusual hobbies, etc. Paradoxically, it appears that while people are *afraid* to be different, they continually *try* to be different. The reason may lie in the fact that the pervasive norm says "be an individual," "express your uniqueness," and yet implicit in that encouragement is the caution: "Don't be *too* different."

An extreme deviant may be labelled (criminal, insane, odd), and his acts may be punished (he may be incarcerated, committed, or isolated). Therefore, when striving to be unique, most people try to do it in socially approved ways, i.e., in ways condoned by the group they identify with and whose norms they adopt.

What does all this have to do with criticism? Criticism often amounts to telling someone that they are not doing what the rest of the world (or their "elite" group) is doing. Criticism says you think the other person is wrong because he is different. "Everyone is wearing flare pants now!"

By criticizing, you make a person feel different. Feeling *too* different is uncomfortable.

A solution is to include yourself or some high status person in the criticism as a fellow part-time deviant. (Be warned, though, that if you set yourself up as Mr. or Ms. Perfection by making a statement like: "Even *I* do that sometimes," your solution will turn into another problem.) Here are a few examples of how the problem may be solved without creating other difficulties.

# You Get What You Ask For

## OBTAINING INFORMATION

Suppose during a very personal conversation when many private fears are being aired, your good friend asks you: "Do you think I'm ugly?" You do think a few pounds could be lost and that his (her) hair and clothing styles could be more up-to-date. You've been wanting to mention this for quite a while, thinking it would help his (her) social life. But while the words say "be honest," the tone says "be gentle." So you quickly reassure your friend: "Don't be silly. . . ."

You and your lover have been having quite a bit of trouble lately. You wonder if the relationship is worth salvaging—so you decide to call some friends to ask their advice.

Call #1: "He's been moody and inconsiderate for months. Nothing I do is right. We fight constantly. Sure he's bright and attractive, but I don't know if I can put up with him any more."

Friend: "Forget it! What do you need all this grief for? Find someone else."

Call #2: "He's everything I ever wanted in a man—bright, generous, attractive, you name it. But lately he's been moody and inconsiderate. Nothing I do is right. We fight constantly. I just don't know what to do."

Friend: "Don't be too hasty. Maybe something's bothering him. I think you should stay with him. Things are bound to work out sooner or later."

You are as confused as ever.

You have just come up with an exciting idea for a psychological experiment and you wish to use your friend as a sounding board.

You: "Hey, Norm, I just had the greatest idea for a study. Listen, the independent variable will be the degree to which I allow the subjects to perceive incongruity between the tachistoscopically presented stimuli and the previously presented warm-up stimuli. The dependent variable is the degree of perceptual distortion as a means of resolving the incongruity as a function of the experimental condition to which the subject has been assigned. I couldn't decide whether to analyze the data in terms of parametric or nonparametric statistics, but I think parametric will allow for maximal utilization of the data and besides is more powerful. What do you think? Isn't that great?"

Norm: "Gee, that sounds great."

You: "Thanks a lot, Norm. I really value your opinion."

In each case, the questioner presumably desired an honest answer. Indeed, an honest answer might have proven quite valuable in telling him how to change so as to achieve his goals. However, the advice-seeker didn't realize how much he biased the answer by the way in which he asked the question and/or the way in which he presented the original information. In each case, the "demand characteristics" prevailed. That is, the reply that the listener thought the person *wanted* to hear was the one that was given—not because it was most accurate, but because it was most accommodating.

We can conceive of situations, as we are sure you can, where the "advice-seekers" are really only interested in being supported in the views they already hold rather than in obtaining additional information. To the extent that they believe it will maximize their future pleasure, we invite them to so indulge.

However, if obtaining information you can rely on is your objective, then some of the strategies we will now discuss are bound to prove helpful.

### The Proof is in the Putting: Phrasing

#### To Sleep, Perchance to . . .

Peter and Sue have been living together for the past eight years. Although they have a great deal of affection for each other and feel they get along quite well, both are dissatisfied with their sex life. From the very start of their relationship they kept this dissatisfaction to themselves so as not to harm what seemed to be an otherwise perfect relationship. Secretly they felt that time and patience would iron out their problems. However the changes over time have been minimal while the frustrations appear to be increasing. Peter and Sue have become the type of people who publicly declare that sex is a minor aspect of a relationship, but who privately yearn for the satisfaction they believe "everyone" else has. Peter and Sue have independently arrived at the conclusion that they are sexually incompatible. This label now dictates their behavior; both are privately, albeit reluctantly, contemplating satisfaction outside of the relationship.

While extra affairs of this type may be congenial to certain people, both Peter and Sue believe that the ramifications of extra curricular activities would be detrimental to their relationship, which they hope to preserve. How might the years of silence and resentment be overcome without resorting to the alternative they find somewhat unacceptable—or is it too late? Obviously, we would not have given this example if they could not go from faking it to making it.

Rather than waiting for your lover to offer personal information without prodding, the information you need is best gotten by asking effective questions. Many people mistakenly think, "If s(he) wanted —————, s(he)'d ask for it."

Yet when people do ask questions, they often do so in such a way that the answer is determined even before the listener has heard the question. When asked, for example, "You didn't like that movie, did you?" it is more difficult to respond "Yes, I did," than "No, of course not." "I enjoy oral sex, don't you?" Here it is easier to say "Yes" than "No." A "Yes" in the first case and a "No" in the second are more effortful and more risky. The question implies that everyone thinks one way; if you think the other, then you are implicitly required to defend your position by giving reasons for your disagreement.

This questioning pattern is a hindrance to obtaining accurate information in a variety of situations, but it is particularly maladaptive in the realm of sexuality. Here there exists a double-edged heightened sensitivity: fear of rejection and fear of hurting someone you love. On many an occasion, either Peter or Sue may have asked questions which, if properly posed, would have opened the field for discussion and subsequent solution. However, when asked incorrectly, the solution becomes more difficult because the true answer has openly been denied.

Imagine yourself being asked the following questions in a love-making situation: "Honey, are you satisfied?", he asks her yawningly. She asks him, "Am I a good lover?" He asks her, "Do you like it when I stimulate you this way?" She asks him, "Is it okay if we don't make love tonight?"

The answer to all of these questions would, when asked tenderly, probably be yes—in spite of the respondent's true feelings. If she said that she wasn't satisfied after he has performed, how is that likely to make him feel? With this thought in mind, she says "Yes." What would her reaction be if the question "Am I a good lover?" were answered in the negative? How would you react? In most cases, it's just easier and less painful to say "Yes."

Back to our hero and heroine.

Peter probably assumed that Sue's answers to his questions were true reflections of her feelings. He was therefore likely to make use of this information in subsequent interactions with her. Sue, on the other hand, continued to be frustrated—perhaps even more so than before—because by giving the false information she kept her displeasure foremost in her thoughts. Similarly, Sue must have assumed that Peter answered her questions truthfully.

Rarely are the answers to yes/no type questions truly informative. If they are asked tenderly, the demand characteristics determine the answer.*

## Forced-Choice Questions

The *forced-choice technique* is characterized by an either/or, rather than yes/no question: "Are you satisfied or would you like me to continue?" "Do you like oral sex more or less than intercourse?" "Do you prefer making love with the light on or with it off?" "Am I being gentle enough or too gentle?"

This technique is useful in a variety of situations: Consider the yes/no question "Jack, do you like my blue dress?" vs. "Jack, which do you like better, my green dress or my blue dress?" The respondent, in this case Jack, is led to believe that he really does have some choice in the matter, and is therefore likely to give some consideration to both alternatives.

* When an air of spite and maliciousness prevails, then an unpleasant answer may be forthcoming. However, in these cases, even when the answer may be true, it is rarely accepted as valid information because the questioner has a handy excuse for discounting it: "S(he) only said that to get back at me for . . ."

Another relevant point is that the less thought an individual gives to a question, the less likely he is to remember that the question was asked. Through the use of forced-choice questions "interchanges" like the following can be avoided.

A man asks his wife who's busy reading the newspaper, "Do you think we should go away this summer?" She answers, "Yes, sure dear" or something to that effect. He starts planning the vacation. Later he mentions it again, asking her a question that requires some thought before answering: "How many days should we plan on taking?" She responds as though she never took part in the earlier conversation. A spat ensues.

### EVERYTHING'S RELATIVE

We all know people who are super-enthusiastic in their descriptions: "That book was the greatest," "That meal was a gourmet's dream," "That joke was the best ever." While it is refreshing to witness such uninhibited delight, you may find it frustrating when you ask such a person for an opinion. But just because an individual is quick to give everything a rave review, you shouldn't conclude that he is incapable of making discriminations. Forced-choice questions may provide a solution. Since his absolute judgments are questionable, ask him to make comparisons. For example, if you ask him to compare two books, one of which you've already read, you can get an idea of whether or not you would enjoy the other.

Q: "Is it as good as *The Unicorn* by Iris Murdoch?"

A: "Well, the author isn't as skillful in building suspense and the characters seem less real, but the plot is ingenious."

In cases like these, asking for a comparison you can evaluate, rather than a straightforward appraisal (e.g., "Did you enjoy it?"), gives you more helpful information.

In the same vein, there are people who have a tendency to put down most things. If a movie is not a cinematographic masterpiece, it is described as having been made by a two-year old. If a play does not reach the heights of Shakespearean grandeur, it was written by chimpanzees who struck typewriter keys at random. According to these people, most things are fashioned by incompetents and forced upon a gullible public. Yet here, too, asking for comparisons may allow you to assess which is the lesser of two evils: "I know none of our restaurants compares to Tour d'Argent in Paris, but which do you prefer, L'Etoile or Copain?"

Since some people are prone to make overwhelmingly positive evaluations and others to make overwhelmingly negative ones, it is important to adjust yourself to the person's style of responding. A good/bad evaluation doesn't tell you what standards were used in arriving at the assessment. If you provide a standard for comparison in your question, the evaluation you receive is of some use.

Poor advice on a movie, a book, or a restaurant can result in wasted time, but rarely does it affect your future in any important way. However, you would probably agree that an evaluation of your work can have serious consequences. The outcome may determine what career you choose, how you view your competence in that field, whether or not you pursue a potentially important idea. Because you have a greater stake in your work, it is all too easy to fall prey to a flattering superlativist or to be shattered by the overly harsh negativist. Thus it is even more important here to know your evaluator's criterion.

Leaving out these extremes, there are still many differences in people's standards. Because certain people are like us in many ways we tend to exaggerate the similarity and think that they are like us in every way. We may mistakenly assume that they use the same criteria as we do in each judgment they make.

Suppose Cheryl asks Maxine "Is your sex life satisfying?" and Cheryl says "Yes." For Cheryl a satisfying sex life may mean intercourse every other night and for Maxine every other week. But if Cheryl believes that Maxine is using the same criterion, she may assume that Maxine has sex about every other night if not more often, and may then be resentful because she and her husband don't.

Suppose Sandy asks Eric, "What did you think of that exam?" and Eric replies, "Oh, I thought it was a snap." Sandy may feel incompetent because she found it to be difficult. However, Eric may consider an easy test one that he can pass, while for Sandy it is one on which she can get an "A."

The forced-choice method of asking questions may indeed be useful in such cases as well, in that it provides you with a mutual basis for comparison.

This strategy is an important one to learn. *It provides the other person with a choice, and you with useful information.*

### PRESENTING A REAL CHOICE

Bart had been in a number of encounter groups. As a result of this experience, he learned to be quite open and honest. Needless to say, his new found pleasure with himself provided him with the confidence to be far bolder than he had ever been.

Bart was in a bar on New York's East Side where he met a very attractive woman who was chatting over cocktails with some friends. They all enjoyed some heavy political conversation for about an hour when Bart had to leave in order to keep another appointment. Later that night Bart called her hoping she'd join him for dinner the following day. She refused. He called twice more and she excused and refused. He called again a few weeks later. This time when she refused, he asked her to be frank with him. He told her that it would save him a good deal of aggravation if she'd just be honest and tell him whether she intended ever to go out with him. She stuck firmly to the excuse she had originally offered. Bart was therefore pretty well convinced that she too was interested. He continued calling and she continued refusing and excusing until finally he had had enough. He called her one last time to tell her off in no uncertain terms.

Bart resented her for leading him on and she resented him for forcing her into an uncomfortable situation. Had he considered how difficult it might have been for her to answer his question honestly and say, "No, I don't want to go out with you," he might have used a different approach.

This set of events is rather typical. People want others to be honest with them, but unwittingly force them into being dishonest. If, before asking, he had thought about the alternatives he gave her, he may have chosen to give her a more comfortable out. For example, "Would you like to go out with me, or would you prefer it if we were friends instead?"

This is likely to occur in most situations where you ask someone for an opinion, especially when you do not know each other all that well. If a negative answer will hurt your feelings, they are likely to distort the truth a bit. "Do you like my new suit?" "Would you like me to make my special broccoli casserole?" "Do you think my painting is any good?" When a truthful answer to your question may be difficult for the respondent to give, give him what he will perceive as a real choice and you will make matters easier for him. "Do you like this suit or the blue one?" "Would you like me to make my broccoli casserole, or should I make string beans?" "Do you think that my painting is any good or should I try sculpting?"

## Open-Ended Questions

Another method for obtaining useful information is the *open-ended question*. This imposes the fewest restrictions on the possible answers that may be given, like essay questions on exams. The answer to the open-ended question "What dress shall I wear?" is likely to be more meaningful than the answer to the yes/no question "Should I wear my blue dress?" With the open-ended question, the respondent has to conjure up at least some of her dresses before he can reply. Since it is just as easy to say red or blue, he is likely to state his *true* preference. In terms of sexual responses, open-ended questions might include "What part of your body is most sensitive?" "When do you most enjoy making love?" "What things excite you most?" "What things annoy you most?"

Of course, all of us use these different ways of asking questions at one time or another. But it is probably done without your being aware of the way you are controlling the answer. By not using these methods, you run the risk of denying yourself the very information you sought. Either the *forced-choice* or *open-ended* questioning methods will enable you to make use of verbal report to increase your knowledge even in the most intimate of situations.

### How an Emotional Investment May Thwart your Interest

No matter how earnest you are about wanting accurate information, there are still going to be people who will refuse to give it if the informative is negative. They will hesitate for fear that their remarks will be painful for you.

The way to get around that barrier is to distance yourself from the information you are seeking. You may accomplish this by speaking of somebody other than yourself as the object of your inquiry.

"John didn't get promoted this year. In general, do you think that means he isn't very good, or is it just as likely to be an oversight?"

"Who do you think has a nicer body, Audrey Hepburn or Sophia Loren?"

"Do you think that Lee's puns make him appear intelligent?"

Unless you've discussed the issue on several occasions before this, or brought up the question from out of the blue, the person is not likely to see the connection between what you are asking and your personal investment. He will then not have to take precautions against hurting your feelings.

There are times people don't give you information you want, not because of your feelings, but rather because of *their* involvement in the issue at hand.

> While at work, a woman was told of a conversation on television. In it, the speaker said that being disloyal is in one's thoughts rather than in one's actions. She found the argument compelling but was not totally convinced. She wondered whether or not her husband felt that a woman who thought about another man while with her husband was more disloyal than a woman who spent time with another man.

> She can't ask her husband outright because he will infer one of two things: either that she is interested in spending time with another man, or that when she's with him, she is thinking about someone else. Needless to say, he would answer in a way that is designed to prevent either of these occurrences rather than express his pure unadulterated opinion.

In order to get an objective answer, she must distance herself from the information she is seeking.

> "At work, Mary wanted to know if I thought someone was more disloyal if they spent time with another person of the opposite sex or if they thought about that person while they were with their spouse. I really hadn't thought about that before. What do you think?"

This technique will not be necessary in most situations. However, it is a good one to keep in mind for those occasions on which emotional investment may get in the way of an honest opinion.

## Deceptive Feedback

In the last two chapters we spoke of getting agreement on some issue so as to enhance the chances of gaining compliance with your ultimate request. You were confident that your position had merit and the point was to try to convince someone else of the same. Now you are not quite as confident, and, although you're still eager for agreement, what you really want is careful consideration of your ideas. That is, you're still interested in the applause, but only as a result of an accurate evaluation of your thoughts.

People often think that their points are coming through loud and clear, when in fact the listener is hopelessly confused. His nods and "um hmms" are misleading polite gestures rather than signs of comprehension. Therefore, the agreement they are getting is not the well-thought-out kind they are seeking. The listener shakes his head yes while saying to himself, "What the hell is he talking about?" Since this has probably been true for you at least on some occasions, it is meaningful to ask why the non-controversial message didn't get through.

Suppose that a person's thinking on an issue has gone through five stages, each of which clarified the last. Now he is ready and eager to share his ideas with an audience. However, all he communicates is the final product. His polite audience is lost.

Unwittingly, he assumed that because the issue was clear to him, it would be clear to them. His failure was forgetting that his listeners had not travelled through the first four stages. This is just what Norm's friend did in the introduction to this chapter when he tried to tell Norm about his research project. He blurted out a very complicated notion in a matter of seconds, when he himself had spent many hours trying to understand and formulate it.

To make matters worse in situations like these, people may generously sprinkle statements like "It's obvious that . . ." or "Clearly then . . ." throughout their conversation. In the face of these statements, it is embarrassing for the audience to ask clarifying questions. This has the effect of defining the listener's task as having to feign understanding in order to appear intelligent. To ask questions would be admitting ignorance about what "should" be obvious to them.

It is "obvious" that just by keeping these points in mind you reduce the likelihood of making the same error. But there are additional precautions to take to ensure that your listener is fully appreciating your message.

*Overview.* While we don't suggest burdening him with all of the steps that led up to your conclusion, it is important that you *begin at the beginning* with some overall, general view of the problem or situation.

*Presentation.* If the person is not quite as familiar as you are with the area under discussion *be sure not to be too technical,* too brief in your description, or to make too many points at once. Unless they are currently using them, abbreviations or code names are stumbling blocks for most people. And even the most sophisticated of listeners has to have a chance to digest your last idea before you fire the next.

*Questions.* The most important point, and a check on your success in keeping your audience with you, concerns the effective use of questions. It is wise to *ask for the listener's thoughts* and opinions all along rather than waiting for an approving answer after a long soliloquy. Questions like "Do you see what I mean?" "Wouldn't you agree?" "Don't you think so?" "Right?" run the risk of occasioning that same false agreement (although they're better than nothing). Open-ended questions like "What do you think about ————?" "How do you feel about ————?" "What are the flaws in my position . . . ?" are more likely to get you answers which reveal the listener's level of understanding and his true appraisal of your position.

*Enthusiasm.* The more excited you sound when you present your position, the less you appear to really want criticism and the more difficult you make it for the person to offer it. Of course, you should show a certain amount of excitement in order to keep your audience in the first place, but after a moderate amount you run a risk. If your listener is sharp enough to notice a flaw, he will be hesitant to point it out for fear of bursting your bubble. Aside from moderating your excitement, it is a good idea to *draw your listener into the excitement* rather than leave him outside as an observer. This can be accomplished by showing enthusiasm about what he may have to offer in addition to your enthusiasm about what you have to say.

This brings up a related issue—involvement. You come to the discussion after being immersed in the issue. In this state, it is difficult to imagine how anybody could fail to be as intrigued. The point is that people don't imagine and are therefore blind to the discrepancy between their own interest and everybody else's. This may explain, in part, why the errors just considered were committed. It may also explain why a number of misattributions are made.

You're getting married and a person you always considered a close friend isn't coming to the wedding reception because of previously made plans to go skiing. You're hurt. You feel that the plans would be broken and the wedding attended if there was any real concern for you.

You're worried about an exam you have to take. Your parents appear to treat it lightly by making remarks like "Oh, it's silly to worry; I'm sure you'll do okay," and "Don't eat so fast; your books can wait a few minutes until you've finished dinner." You get annoyed at them for not understanding what you're going through. You may think they're being condescending and that they're treating you like a little kid.

In both of these dramas, the main characters suffered more than was necessary. In addition, the villains were labeled too harshly. The more time you spend on something, the more involved you become. Since the friend and the parents have not spent the same amount of time thinking about the particular issues, it is unfair to expect their involvement to equal yours. Because of the different levels of involvement of each of the characters, the information available was misread. Being less involved is then easily confused with being unconcerned.

After the event is over, there is an immediate drop in involvement and, as time passes, it decreases even more. As you become more distant from the issue yourself, it is easier to re-establish the old relationship. However, because of the initial misunderstanding, you may still feel you were wronged, even though you were big enough to forgive. The next time you are tempted to play the martyr, or think somebody doesn't care about you, or accuse somebody of being inconsiderate, *the different levels of involvement of you and your listener should be called to mind.*

Once you have this understanding of interpersonal interactions, you can combat the problem in yet another way. That is, simply by increasing the other person's involvement in the matter of concern to you. By sharing the details of the experience, the joys, the pains, the importance of the occasion, all along the way, people cannot help but become more involved.

## The Advice You Get May Be Your Own

Remember the woman at the beginning of the chapter who called her friends for advice on her love life? If you are an acute observer you probably noticed something of interest. The advice she received depended very much on the information she gave.

In the first telephone conversation she emphasized the trouble and heartache her lover was causing. Consequently, she was advised to forget him. When she emphasized his assets in the second conversation and hinted that the trouble was recent and possibly temporary, she was told to reconsider.

While the difference in her statements is clear to us, it probably was not to her. She no doubt thought that the conflicting advice she received was a result of the difference between her two friends. Either the first friend dislikes him and the second does not, the first friend is discriminating and the second is too optimistic, or the first is a pessimist, while the second is perceptive. Whatever the case, she was likely to attribute the difference to them rather than to herself.

Naturally, the two friends might hold different views to begin with. One might believe that there are many fish in the sea, so cast your line elsewhere. The other may think it's a bad season, stick with what you've got. But even so, they are listening to what she is telling them, and they are most certainly influenced by it. The information she selects to communicate is the information they are most likely to use.

Few people realize two of the most important factors that go to make up the advice other people give you.

(1) For the most part, in your personal matters, *people know only what you've already told them.* That means that the advice you are getting is largely your own. Thus, if you've told your friend at home odious things about a person at work and later ask whether or not they think it's a good idea for you to go out with him (her), you are not receiving the objective opinion you might have thought.

(2) The second, and perhaps more important, factor is that *people usually tell you what they think you want to hear.* Sometimes they are no more aware than you are that this is taking place. At other times, they assume that you've already made up your mind and are really only asking for confirmation.

Let's assume that while confirmation would be nice, you are again really seeking unbiased information. What do you do?

If an argument between you and your partner has just taken place when you ask for advice, your impulse might be to tell your side of the story only. Indeed, that may be the way you see it at that time and your momentary desire is for sympathy and support. Stifle yourself. Present both viewpoints to the listener, giving *more* emphasis to the other side.

One obvious consequence is that the advice they give you will

be more meaningful and more helpful, since it will take account of more information. The other person, able to see the situation more dispassionately than you, may see a resolution to the problem that you had not thought of. He may have had a similar experience and can give you the benefit of his having lived through it. He may be able to calm you down so that you can resolve it yourself. It is the rare person who, when asked for sympathy, will solicit the information about the other side that will enable him to form a more objective opinion. Since you will get what you ask for, the more responsibility you take for presenting a balanced picture and the more information you share, the better the feedback.

Another point to consider seriously, is that in the process of presenting both sides you may very well come to see the merits of your "opponent's" position. You may feel foolish starting out by huffing and puffing about the unfair treatment you have received and ending up by realizing your part in it. But your listener is more likely to admire your willingness to admit error than to chide you for changing your mind. Moreover, the realization that your partner isn't that rotten after all is far more valuable than the temporary satisfaction of feeling that you are right.

Now, for a moment, think of the position you are putting your advisor in by giving a one-sided account. Imagine how he feels after he has vigorously supported your position, has proclaimed your partner a bastard unworthy of you, and has strongly recommended you split with him (her)—and then you and your partner happily get back together. How will he feel in your presence? Probably rather foolish. How will you feel in his? How will you feel about him? Probably unkindly—after all, he has expressed dislike for someone you are very fond of.

Think of the position you might be putting yourself in, even if you don't end up reunited. Your listener has heard only your side, has agreed with you, and has given you advice based on the information you have provided. Suppose he then hears the other side from your partner. It will immediately become clear to him that your account was one-sided, and when it does, he will begin

to regret the advice he so obligingly offered. The more he resents having been used, the more he will accept the second version—even if it is just as lop-sided as yours. As he fits his information into the new framework, you become the loser.

Therefore, in the interest of meaningful feedback, your own objectivity, and consideration for your listener and yourself, our advice is to consider and present the other side as accurately as you possibly can.

### If It Hurts, It Must Be the Truth:
### Assessing Unfavorable Feedback

There is a belief that pervades our society: the notion that negative information is more likely to be true than positive information. Consequently, we find that unfavorable feedback is readily accepted as accurate,* while favorable feedback is often questioned and dismissed as either faulty judgment, partiality, or an attempt to ingratiate or manipulate. The bearer of ill-tidings is credited with insight into the real you, although you are far from appreciative. The complimenter is seen as "just trying to be nice" or is faulted for his poor perception, lack of discrimination, or his selfish interests.

> Carl tells Patty he thinks she's beautiful. She doesn't accept it at face value because of all the possible ulterior motives he may have for complimenting her: "He wants to sleep with me," "He want to be complimented himself," "He wants me to like him," "He wants to borrow money," "He must want something."
>
> Things are different when Jim tells Patty that although she's plain, there's something very attractive about her. All she hears is plain, and is too willing to believe it. After all, if it weren't true, why else would he say it? She's then likely to harbor the insult and nurse

* In our discussion of criticism we said that flatly stated criticism may be rejected. We meant that in a behavioral sense. That is, the person is not likely to change as a result of it, at least not initially. However, the information conveyed is often believed to be true.

it until it grows all out of proportion. The situation in which it occurred becomes ambiguous as Jim becomes the whole world looking at her and wincing.

Similarly, the person who gives a poor prognosis or who prophesies doom is more likely to be believed than one who paints a rosier picture. Pessimism is equated with realism, while optimism is equated with naive idealism. Perhaps this is accurate in the realm of world politics, but it is neither accurate nor adaptive in personal politics.

Advice on a deteriorating relationship:

Negative: "I've seen this happen before. Take it from me, I've been through it. Once this begins, it's all downhill. Get out now."

This is seen as wise advice based on experience.

Positive: "Don't worry. It will all work out. Most couples have their bad moments. Stick with it."

This is seen as glib and hollow advice designed to comfort you.

Favorable feedback, however, need not reflect an attempt at ingratiation or a feeble effort to buoy your spirits despite the "reality" of the situation. It is often the case that the person is offering an honest appraisal of a quality he appreciates. Perhaps the fact that this does not occur often enough tempts people to discount it when it does.

When giving undue credence to unfavorable feedback, people often overlook the fact that insults or pessimistic advice may be products of ulterior motives as well: the person is trying to get back at you for something you did; he had a bad day and needs a scapegoat; putting you down makes him feel superior; you treat him with more respect after he gives you negative information, etc. Therefore, it is foolhardy to assume that unfavorable feedback must be true and positive feedback is most likely to be false. If there is no additional evidence, it is best to assume the positive (see Chapter 1). If there is some other external validation for the negative, keep it in proper perspective. Patty didn't. If she believed Jim, she should have realized that this was one man's view and not the world's. Then she could decide whether she should change her hairstyle, her clothes, or the like, in order to please him or the few others who think as he does. It is too easy to overgeneralize from one person's remarks to the rest of the population.

We need not emphasize again how the beliefs you hold may become self-fulfilling prophecies. If you believe negative things about yourself or pessimistic advice about your situation, and subsequent events support this view, do not use this as evidence for the accuracy of your assessment. Had you believed the opposite, instead, it too might have come to pass.

### Ignorance in the Pursuit of Knowledge is No Vice

Many people believe at some level that admitting ignorance on an issue will be taken as a sign of general ignorance. The higher the status of a person, the more he feels he "should" know everything. While a student or a beginner in a profession feels entitled to ask questions, a professor or an executive often thinks he must have all the answers. At times even the novice may feel compelled to give the impression that his storehouse of knowledge is complete in order to make a good impression.

This mask of omniscience often stands in the way of asking for the advice you need. Instead you may choose to grope in the dark, wasting time and energy at the expense of your finished product. Later, you may resort to shifting the blame to the incompetence of your colleagues, the lack of resources at your disposal, or, oddly enough, the absence of good advice, when the result is not as good as it could be.

This fear of appearing incompetent interferes with getting good advice even when advice is requested.

The pattern seems to go something like this:

(1) Don't approach the person who's most likely to have the answer first if he's your superior, because he'll think you're stupid.

(2) Don't ask the "real" question—ask for clarification of a small point and hope he will answer your question in the process.

(3) Ask so as to get agreement, not further information.

(4) Make believe you understand right away, even though you don't.

(5) If the person doesn't provide the information you were looking for, probe no further.

(6) If you've changed your mind and want to ask him now, change it back again because now he's probably sure you know the answer already and you'll prove your incompetence beyond a shadow of a doubt.

You need advice on how to write up a report on an advertising campaign. You have to verify several assumptions you've made about consumers, but feel you should have this information at your fingertips. First you look at the written material available, but you can't find what you're looking for. Then you go over to Harold's desk to see if he can help. Harold is a member of the art department and as such is not likely to have the answers to your technical questions, but at least you're not too embarrassed to ask him. Harold couldn't help, and you're beginning to get really anxious about the issue. The next stop is Ben's desk. Ben is in your department, and, while senior to you, he is not your boss. You ask, "Isn't it true that . . ." He answers, "Yes, but you have to remember . . ." You nod in agreement even though you haven't the slightest idea what he is talking about. But you think to yourself that you'll have to find some other way. Now you really feel stupid. Since you won't ask your boss, there seems to be no way to get the information. How can you go back and ask Ben to explain what he meant when you stood there smiling and nodding while he tried to explain it before?

The purpose of that vignette, well seasoned with sarcasm, was to point out all of the time and energy people waste. The problem stems from one false premise—that others think less of you for asking questions. This is not so, especially when you ask your question with some confidence or provide some explanation:

"Ben, I have to make out a report on the last advertising campaign, but to do it accurately I've got to check some facts. Do you happen to know what . . ."

"I'm not sure I understand you correctly. Are you saying that . . ."

"I've been away from this for a long time—do you happen to recall . . ."

Asking a question means you don't know a particular answer. There is no crime in that. However, if you are discovered pretending to know an answer you do not know, your entire storehouse of knowledge will be called into question.

Before you feel too foolish about requesting some information, think about how you would react if someone asked you a similar question. Chances are you'd help him as best you could and give the interaction no further thought. Why then should you expect less from others?

We hope that by now we have sufficiently convinced you that being persuasive, obtaining compliance, and getting valid information are not chance happenings. Other people's reactions very much depend on you—the way you plan, package, and present what you have to say. Your increased understanding of interpersonal politics now enables you to be sensitive to subtle controlling factors. Your influence over these controlling factors allows you to determine the outcome in difficult situations that you might have thought were beyond your control. All that is left for the strategies we've discussed to be effective is their use.

# A POST-SCRIPT TO THE LAST THREE CHAPTERS: SELF-PERSUASION

Many of the techniques that increase your influence in interpersonal situations may also be used to persuade yourself when you are reluctant to comply with your own wishes. Here are just a few examples.

### Public Commitment

We spoke of public commitment before in the discussion of how you may get help by stating your request in the presence of an observer. It was dealt with even more directly in "obligating in advance." It was there that we explained the effect of *time* on your attitude toward a favor you were asked to do: although initially eager for an event to occur, as the time of the event approaches your desire to avoid the issue increases.

How might this be helpful when applied to yourself? If you

make a decision to do something but keep this to yourself, you can always change your mind at the last minute. You might want to back out because, as the time to implement your decision grows nearer, the disadvantages for carrying out the choice grow clearer. However, if you publicly committed yourself by disclosing your decision—that is, *obligated yourself in advance* —it would be much more difficult to back out. Keep in mind that you knew the disadvantages when you first made your decision and that the advantages clearly outweighed them.

> Bud thinks he deserves a raise in salary. His boss is an unpredictable person with a rather violent temper. Nevertheless, Bud has tentatively decided to ask him for what he sees as an equitable exchange for his hard work. His boss is on vacation until the end of the week, so Bud will have to wait until then. In the meantime, his reasons for wanting the increase are having trouble remaining in first place ahead of his fear of the reaction it might occasion in the ogre. Now that the time has finally come, Bud has reconsidered. Perhaps he'll wait until tomorrow. . . .

Let's go back for a moment to the time when Bud first made the decision to ask for the raise. Suppose he now discussed his decision with his friends and family. He presented his side of the argument and succeeded in convincing everyone he spoke to of how deserving he was. Now when his boss returns, and he considers backing down, he must reconsider, "What will I tell all my friends if I don't ask?" So Bud makes his request and thinks more of himself for having done so.

### Channeling your Thoughts

In the same way that the information you give to other people influences their reaction, the information you choose to emphasize to yourself determines your reaction in a given situation. The workings of this process may clearly be seen in the realm of sexuality.

While sex is generally regarded as an all-consuming activity, too often other factors intrude to inhibit the consummation. Sex is not just a physiological response. The information you attend to and the mental sets and attitudes you bring to the love-making situation are of paramount importance. These may fall into at least three categories:

(1) Thoughts and feelings about your partner.
(2) Thoughts about external circumstances.
(3) Preoccupation with your own performance.

If a person is thinking, "S(he) is using me," "All s(he) cares about is sex," "It's going to be the same old thing tonight," "S(he) never cares about my satisfaction," "Who is s(he) thinking about now?" "Why didn't s(he) shave?" etc., then participation in and enjoyment of the sexual act will be greatly reduced.

Ponderings about external circumstances will result in the same loss of sexual appetite. "I wonder if the kids are asleep," "What if my parents catch us?" "That dripping faucet is driving me crazy," "We're going to be late to the dinner."

Preoccupation with your own performance can also be a problem. The bedroom is unfortunately often used as the proving ground for one's competence as a fe(male). It is possible for one to become so ego-involved that sexual satisfaction is almost completely sacrificed for the desire to pass the test. Sexual satisfaction decreases and anxiety increases as your perception of your partner goes from sensitive lover to critical judge. Your concern may be manifest in such statements as: "Am I as good as her (his) last lover?," "Will I be able to climax" "Will I bring my lover to orgasm?" Since anxiety inhibits sexual responsiveness, worrying about passing the test may be the one reason you fail.

What *should* you think about in order to maximize your pleasures? Before making love you might try thinking of all the nice things about your lover (those things that attracted you in the first place) and all the positive things s(he) has done for you lately. This may sound like advice from Pollyanna, but who says that something has to be complex to be true? All we can do is urge you to try it and assess its benefits for yourself.

During the act, attend to those things that excite you most. This may be a particular part of the body, a particular sexual response, or an image of the total act itself—whatever turns you on.

It requires a bit of practice to make the transition from those distracting thoughts to thoughts which focus on the positive aspects of your lover and the act. But this is one situation in which the practice is minimal while the payoff is great.

Naturally, selecting and focusing on positive information is useful in any situation where the aspects you are now dwelling on are preventing you from recognizing and achieving what is in your best interest.

## CALMING IMAGERY

Have you ever had the experience of talking to someone who makes you feel nervous and incompetent either because of his status or his confident manner?

Most of us have at some time been in the position where our anxiety and fear of negative judgment have indeed prevented us from showing ourselves to best advantage. We might have clammed up, drawn a blank, or put our foot in our mouths because of the other thoughts running through our heads in the presence of this frightening figure. Then there is the snowball effect. With each meeting we became more nervous, remembering the last disastrous encounter.

We are assuming that you've tried telling yourself he's just another person like you, not a god, that he too was once in your position, etc.—but that the good sense of these statements didn't succeed in calming you down.

How can you overcome this? The better your visual imagery is, the more successful you'll be. The goal is to bring your exaggerated image of a superhuman back into the proper perspective. Think of some of the most mundane behaviors virtually all people have committed, like belching, passing wind, or struggling with irregularity. Now choose one of these actions and imagine your immaculate person engaging in it. Make the image as vivid as possible, but don't laugh out loud because he won't understand why you're so amused (and you don't want to be in the position of having to tell him). This should put you at ease. When you are feeling more in control of the situation than you did before, you'll, of course, forgive him his momentary lapse.

The assumption is that when you yourself are cool and confident, you will become more effective in the situation.

If the relationship is one that will continue, once you've established yourself and become more relaxed with the person, there will no longer be any need for such imaginative imagery.

### Questioning Yourself

In the last chapter we considered the different ways of asking questions so as to obtain information from others. What about the questions you pose to yourself? Does it make any difference which way you ask them? Just as the type of question you ask someone else will tell him what to attend to, the questions you ask yourself will determine what you focus on. A brief example should suffice.

You're faced with a difficult task—figuring out the answer to a complex problem, repairing an appliance, conquering a new skill. The solution is not immediately clear. What do you ask yourself? Too many people ask themselves "Can I do it?" Too many of these people respond "No." Those that reply "Maybe" reserve the right to resign at any time. The amount of effort you are willing to expend, however, is closely related to how confident you are that the effort will pay off. Therefore a "maybe" answer leads to a so-so effort.

If, on the other hand, your question is "*How* can I do it?" you're set to find an answer. You bypass the questioning of your abilities and concentrate on finding the most promising strategy. This additional focus on the task rather than on yourself may lead you to

Drawing by O. Soglow; © 1972 The New Yorker Magazine, Inc.

appreciate different aspects of the problem which may be critical to its solution. With this outlook, if your first approach fails, you have a partial answer to your "How do I do it?" question, i.e., "Not this way." Instead of being a blow to your confidence, each miss can, in a sense, be seen as bringing you closer to the solution by allowing you to eliminate one more incorrect strategy.

Aside from these suggestions, many of the techniques of persuasion used to gain compliance from others can also be used on yourself. You no doubt talk to yourself more than to anyone else. Why not make this dialogue work to your advantage?

# Dangers When We Meet

## IMPRESSIONS

It would be a terrible burden to have to worry about the impact of each action and statement on other people. It would probably take all the pleasure out of relationships. For example, imagine obsessing over whether Mr. X thinks your "Good morning" conveyed the proper degree of friendliness. There are situations, however, where extra thought is necessary—where it's important that you be thought well of.

Some people think it displays great confidence to assert that they don't care what others think. If this means that they can't be concerned with what *everyone* thinks, that's fine. But if it means that they don't care what *anyone* thinks, that's foolish.

For some, this seeming nonchalance may serve to cover what they see as their inability to control other people's impressions of them.

Others who make this assertion falsely equate concern about other people's impressions with a preoccupation with "appearances" or exaggerated concern over keeping up with the Joneses. There is an important point that they do not recognize. While they may not be worried about approval from the "establishment," they are indeed concerned with the opinions of their peer group.

Other people's impression of us largely determines how they behave toward us, which in turn determines how we react to them. Our impression of others exerts a similar influence.

We all have very definite ideas about most people we meet. Where do these ideas come from? What maintains them? And how can they be changed? In the process of answering these questions we will do battle with widespread beliefs about the nature of personality—the idea that an individual's personality is

made up of a number of basic traits which explain his behavior; the idea that forming impressions or assessing someone's personality amounts to discovering and evaluating these traits.

We will begin with a discussion of labels for, after all, what is a *trait* but a *label* we give to people?

## What's in a Name? Labels and Stereotypes

Does a rose by any other name smell as sweet? While it would be comforting to think so, we must take issue with Shakespeare on this point. His statement implies that no matter what a thing is called, its essential qualities will still shine through. We maintain that names or labels create cognitive sets which can transform our sensory experience.

Names and labels serve the purpose of organizing our thoughts, directing our senses to pick up certain cues but not others, and determining our interpretation of those cues. They are usually helpful because they allow us to know a great deal about a person, place, or thing on the basis of limited information. If you tell me you have an apple in the bag you are holding, I can tell you many things about it without seeing it because of the past experience I have had with other things that bear the same name.

In the sense that a label tells us what to expect, calling a flower "skunkweed" instead of "rose" may set us to look for negative characteristics, may result in our focusing on the thorns, and may lead us to conclude that it is not a very appropriate Valentine's Day gift.

About five years ago, when one of the authors was in Europe, an uncommon common event occurred. It was uncommon because it doesn't happen to most people very often and common because so many of us have experienced it at one time or another. When people travel, they often allow themselves to be more adventurous than they usually are at home. They take more risks in the people they meet, in the activities they try out, and in the foods they sample. It is food with which this story is concerned.

It was in a small restaurant in Rome. After having gorged myself with pasta for the past few days, my clothes and I decided that I needed a change. Although it wasn't a culinary delight, there was a dish on the menu that fit the bill. It was described as a mixed grill—steak, liver, chicken, veal, and pancreas. I was hoping that there would be plenty to eat so I could casually avoid the last. When the dinner was served, one of the people with me pointed out which item on the plate was the pancreas. I thought to myself that I was being foolish. "I never tried it, maybe I'll like it." There seemed no good reason why I should like all the other meats and get sick at just the thought of eating pancreas. So, I was going to force myself.

I first ate the other meat so that I would not begin the venture on an empty stomach. They were all fairly tasty. Then the moment of truth arrived. The first biteful was the hardest. It stuck in my throat as if to punish me for my decision. But I wasn't going to let it get the best of me. I took another taste. While the chore wasn't getting any easier, there was comfort in knowing that the battle was soon to be over. "If I hold my breath while I down the last gulp, the victory is mine."

Although the pancreas lay at the pit of my stomach, I put a feather in my cap for the minor triumph.

You may ask whether the point of this is that I probably could have enjoyed the pancreas if it had another name. Not only is that the point, but that was indeed the case. As I was in the process of congratulating myself for the feat, my friend informed me that he was teasing me earlier. I was actually feeling sick when I was eating chicken, one of my favorite foods, and enjoyed the pancreas thinking it was another piece of liver.

Although we've begun with a discussion of roses and pancreas, what we are really concerned with are people. Just as names affect the psychological experience of flowers and food, so too do labels affect your perception of individuals. If a person is a reformed criminal or has returned to society from the back ward of some mental institution, and if he still wears the label, no matter how much like everybody else he may now be, he will be reacted to differently. If a person who gives large sums of money freely to friends is described to you as a "squanderer," your impression upon meeting the individual is likely to be quite different from what it would be if he were labeled "philanthropist."

Below are descriptions of two people. Try to imagine what each person is like. Consider such things as what it would be like to have a friend like this, a relative, a classmate, or a co-worker. Do this for one before going on to the next.

James is a very cold person. People who know him describe him as ambitious, determined, skillful, critical, and practical. He has always been quite successful in his pursuits, academically and professionally.

John is a very warm person. People who know him describe him as ambitious, determined, skillful, critical, and practical. He has always been quite successful in his pursuits, academically and professionally.

It is clear that both descriptions are identical except for the initial adjective (Asch, 1946). The rest of the description, however, is not perceived in the same way for both people. Rather our set to see one as cold and the other warm decidedly colors our reaction to the remaining characteristics. For James, "ambitious" takes on overtones of "cut-throat." "Determined" seems to connote "pushy" and inconsiderate of others. "Skillful" is seen as sly or crafty. "Critical" and "practical" mean scornful and selfish. For John, on the other hand, the same adjectives give us the picture of a well-adjusted, well-liked person who is motivated, competent, discriminating, and sensible.

Now suppose we change the second description to read:

Mary is a very warm person. People who know her describe her as ambitious, determined, skillful, critical, and practical. She has

147

always been quite successful in her pursuits, academically and professionally.

The first word alerts us to the sex of the person being described. This creates a certain set of expectations against which the person is likely to be evaluated. While we may still be influenced by the word "warm," it does not direct our perception of the other adjectives as strongly as it did with John. Unfortunately, a woman is expected to be passive, accepting, and domestic. If she is said to be a competent and independent professional, there is something wrong. To make it right she must be seen as "unfeminine." Mary may be viewed as poorly adjusted or deviant, although John, with the identical characteristics, is seen as precisely the opposite.

Thus, the initial names and labels cause us to interpret new information in a different light. They may be seen as the first pieces in a puzzle—ones which lead us to guess what the rest is like. The tendency is to complete the picture in our minds with qualities which seem to go together. Then, in order for the picture to remain consistent or plausible, we interpret the additional pieces of information so they fit with what we already know.

## DAFT OR DEFT?

Suppose you were told that the following fragment was written by a psychotic.

*"A Mounted Umbrella"*
What was the use of not leaving it there where it would hang what was the use if there was no chance of ever seeing it come there and show that it was handsome and right in the way it showed it. The lesson is to learn that it does show it, that it shows it and nothing, that there is nothing, that there is no more to do about it and just so much more is there plenty of reason for making an exchange.

You might call this a "word salad." The words are mixed up, the train of thought is not continuous, and the whole does not seem coherent. While you probably made some attempt to decipher it, it might soon have seemed clear that this was a product of a deeply troubled person, a person with little control over his thoughts. Your reaction was most likely one of alarm and pity.

However, if you were told that this passage is from a well-known work of Gertrude Stein,* which in fact it is, your response would most certainly change. Although it still might not be your literary cup of tea, you would know that the author was very much in control. The product would now be seen as creative, provocative, amusing, and challenging. Accordingly, you would spend more time trying to tune into the style, follow the line of reasoning, and appreciate the message. If you failed to make sense of it, you would more likely question your own sensitivity than the writer's sanity.

## DEVIL OR ANGEL?

In the same vein, what if an English teacher received something like the above passage from a student in fulfilment of a creative writing assignment. Would he call it a creative success and give it an "A," or would he view it as unintelligible nonsense?

To a large extent, his reaction will depend on his prior impression of the student. If the teacher thinks the student is very intelligent and highly original, he would tend to approach this piece of work with a favorable set. He might then respond with great interest to its novel form and content and spend much time considering its merits. The phenomenon here is known as the "halo effect." It refers to the fact that a person who is seen as "good" is surrounded by a positive "aura"—all of his words and deeds are viewed in this light.

* From *Selected Writings of Gertrude Stein*, Carl Van Vediten (ed.) (New York: Random House, 1962), p. 469.

On the other hand, if the teacher considers the student to be dull and unimaginative, he would be rather reluctant to give him the benefit of the doubt. He might see the novelty as a reflection of grammatical ignorance, stylistic incompetence, and intellectual confusion. As a result, he would probably cover the paper with red marks and comments about sentence construction and punctuation. We might dub this phenomenon the "pitchfork effect"—a person is seen in negative terms and the positive aspects of his actions are obscured by this shadow.

### A Dubious Distinction

Is a person who greets you with little enthusiasm snobbish or shy? Is a person who remains aloof in the midst of a heated discussion cold, bored, or insecure? Is an acquaintance who asks many questions about your personal life prying or concerned?

In the absence of further information, it is impossible to conclude what lies behind a person's behavior in any situation. However, you can be sure that the labels you choose to describe that behavior will determine how you react to the person.

> Your advisor repeatedly asks how your project is coming along. You label this curiosity and see the question as a reflection of his interest in you and excitement over your work. You're grateful, eager to give him all the details, and quick to ask his advice when necessary. Now, assume that you labelled his inquisitiveness as distrust of your competence. You see his questioning as snooping and view him as pushy. You avoid him. You restrain yourself from bringing the details or the difficulties of the work to him because you expect him to be too judgmental.

Things like this happen all the time. In fact, the realization that there are labels which have different connotations but describe the same thing may clear up yet another mystery. The assignment of different labels may partly explain the "to each his own" phenomenon. That is, one man's poison may be another man's passion, not because of his love of the deadly, but because of the more positive alternative label he has assigned.

Jill is a rather elegant sophisticate, well poised and charming. Although generally happy with herself, she is presently bemoaning a deficiency. It appears that her boyfriend's old girl friend was, in Jill's words, "a top notch creative cook," whereas Jill's expertise is in the area of frozen food.

Monica is a very pretty young woman who is approximately the same age as Jill. She succeeds in conveying the same impression upon first meeting. They share yet another similarity. Monica is also all thumbs in the kitchen. However, to her this implies that she has more important things to do.

While both were at a small dinner party given by a friend, one of the guests remarked on what a good cook their hostess was. Monica seized the opportunity to comment, "You really are a good cook. I didn't know you were so domestic."

A creative person is someone both Jill and Monica admire, while a domestic person in their eyes is someone worthy of sympathy.

Thus it is important to read your label carefully, for the ingredients that go into your choosing that label may just as easily be given another name. The directions contained on the different labels may dictate very different behaviors.

Think of all the people you don't like. What don't you like about them? Are they too aggressive, petty, selfish, or stubborn? Do you think you might dislike them less if you labelled their behavior assertive, exacting, insecure, or confident?

### Traitors to the Cause: Assigning Traits

Okay, you say, so it's possible, on first meeting someone, to mistake shyness for snobbishness. What's so terrible about that? Assuming you are careful to keep an open mind, further interactions should tell you what the person is "really like." You may argue that when you know a person better, *then* you can accurately identify his underlying traits.

People freely assign personality traits to others. These are what we might call some of the labels we've just discussed like "aggressive," "stubborn," or "shy." Some view these as labels for deep-seated enduring traits. After all, if some characteristic is so much a part of a person, doesn't it make sense to give it a name? This is just the point we want to take issue with here. Are personality traits part of a person? In fact, do they really exist at all?

Personal experience makes us very reluctant to question the existence of traits. When observing other people's behavior it appears that there are indeed broad, deeply ingrained characteristics which drive them to behave in certain ways. We then assume that they will act in these ways regardless of external circumstances. Indeed, the term "trait" implies that the reaction is almost exclusively a function of the *person* and not of the *situation*.

We, too, were skeptical at first. But the psychological findings that have accumulated over recent years have provided overwhelming support for an alternative position. What we call personality has now been shown to be largely dependent upon the specific situation the person is in. Whether a person behaves honestly or dishonestly, passively or aggressively, impulsively or reflectively, or dependently or independently, depends very much on the task he is performing, how he interprets it, who is present, what the consequences are, and the like. There has been little evidence to support the notion that there are fixed traits that follow people around from situation to situation.

Certainly there are individual differences in the way people interpret and react to situations. They have learned different patterns of behavior since their childhood. However, these individual differences are, to a large extent, very much exaggerated by us when we are observing others, simply because we tend to ignore situational influences. When *we* do something negative ourselves, we are usually very quick to see that the cause of our behavior lies partly in the social environment—"When did they put the garbage can over there? I walked into it because I didn't know it had been moved," "The teacher said that if I didn't pass that test I'd be thrown out of school—I had to cheat," "I only yelled like that because he was trying to take advantage of me." The only time we see ourselves as clumsy, dishonest, or nasty individuals is if we have had previous doubts in those areas. Otherwise, we see the circumstances of the situation as responsible. On the other hand, when we observe others committing the same behaviors, we are prone to attribute the causes to underlying traits. "Now there goes a clumsy person," "That guy's a cheater from the word go," "I wouldn't like to meet him in a dark alley."

What are some common instances in which people are prone to assign traits? Why are the situational variables ignored?

*Counter-normative or inappropriate behavior.* When the person's behavior seems counter-normative or inappropriate and the situational justification is not immediately obvious, we postulate traits to explain the action.

Picture the following situations and imagine what your impression would be if you came upon each yourself.

A person singing loudly—with friends at a party; alone in the subway; in the shower.

A person curled up on a chair reading a book—at a party; at home alone; at home with an exceptionally attractive member of the opposite sex.

A person comes up to you and asks if you can spare a dime—the person is a man in tattered clothing; a well-dressed man carrying a briefcase; a sensuous woman.

While the other two vocalists are seen as normal, the lone singer in the subway is undoubtedly "out of his mind," for what possible situational circumstances could explain this? But wait a minute. What if he were pledging a fraternity and was required to do this as part of his initiation? What if he were a social psychologist testing whether or not people avoid you when you do unusual things? Or, what if he were from another culture where singing on trains is common?

Our reader is fine when at home alone but may be an antisocial or an asexual person in the other two instances. But here too there can be perfectly logical explanations. Suppose his roommate appeared with a lively group of friends, and he had an exam the next day. Surely you would understand his studying. Or what if it were a book of party games? How about the person who insists on reading despite the beautiful scenery? What if that attractive person were a relative or a person with whom a fight has just taken place?

Lastly, let's consider the three "beggars." Excuses are easily made for the second man—he must have lost his wallet. However, the first is seen as a lazy and shiftless hobo who probably never owned a wallet. And the third is given a label that implies she is soliciting more than your dime. Couldn't the first excuse be true for the others as well?

Thus, when it is easy to explain a behavior by attaching a label to the person, we don't look very hard for alternative situational explanations.

**Consistent behavior over time and across situations.** Take the person who always seems the same to you. Let's say he's consistently domineering. It's not just you—he seems to push everyone at work around. Suppose you met him at a party where he didn't know anyone else. It might be embarrassing for you to then introduce your spouse to the man you described as a domineering bastard, when now he seems like such a docile pussycat.

You might be saying, "You're wrong, there *are* traits—because I know a guy who's the same at both parties and work." We do not concede. *You* might be that situational influence. Suppose that for some reason this person is trying to impress *you* and for him that means "be domineering." You might see him act this way in situation after situation; however, he may be a very different person in your absence. If the situations you are comparing are similar, it is not surprising that his behavior is consistent.

What about the man who behaves irresponsibly every time and every place you meet him. Not only that, but all your friends have confirmed your impression. He disappears for days at a time, leaving his family to fend for themselves. He spends money carelessly. He agrees to favors he never fulfills. You can't count on him for anything.

You might ask how can we possibly understand his behavior in terms of the external circumstances? Let's look at the external circumstances. Here is a person whom people find very attractive and warm up to immediately. All it takes is an apology and a smile for his irresponsible actions to be forgiven. These actions rarely cost him very much. He knows no harm will come to his family because his well-to-do in-laws will step in to help each time he steps out. Whenever he shirks his responsibilities, others assume them for him. Thus, every time things get rough for him, the payoffs lie in escaping to greener pastures.

Now suppose the situation were changed so that his actions that were rewarded before were now punished. People stopped forgiving him and covering up for his misdeeds. You can be sure a change in his behavior would follow. He would then appear to be a very different person.

*Violation of the "just world" hypothesis.* Another reason for assigning traits may be understood in terms of the "just world" hypothesis. This involves the assumption that the world is fair, the people in it are equitable, and everyone gets what he deserves. Although some may see life as a fight for survival, they would still maintain that the fittest survive—that those who earn it, make it. In this process of natural selection, only the undeserving are weeded out. If a misfortune befalls a person, he is seen as somehow having brought it on himself through his carelessness, incompetence, dishonesty, or immorality.

It would be very uncomfortable for people to live in a world where personal disasters or painful events occurred by chance. There would be no sense of security. Imagine believing that despite your talent, hard work, and clean living, you could wake up some day and find that your career dreams have been shattered, your family has left you, and your friends want nothing more to do with you. The anxiety would be close to unbearable. Besides this discomfort, what would be the point of working for anything if you could be robbed of it so easily and through no fault of your own? But if you believe that bad things only happen to "bad" people you will rest assured that as long as you watch out, you'll be safe.

Thus, for reasons of personal security, people do not want to assume that outcomes are due to chance. Instead, to understand events, they make trait attributions. These are usually the only alternatives that are considered. Since people are not used to seeking out situational determinants of other people's fortunes or misfortunes, this rarely becomes a choice. But in view of what we have previously discussed, seeking situational determinants should now be seen as the most sensible choice. Understanding the circumstances surrounding an event frees us from the fear that events are unpredictable and, at the same time, prevent us from engaging in unnecessary name-calling.

When we assign a trait name to an individual's behavior, we are accepting that behavior as a given. We are saying he is stubborn, for example, in the same way we say he is blue-eyed or 5′ 8″ tall. By assigning traits we are defining the person and definitions are, by meaning, limiting. To say that somebody is something says he cannot be something else. Thus, if we say that a man is a domineering person, that means he cannot be passive or submissive. But if we talk about his behaving in a domineering way at work, we leave open the possibility that he may behave differently in other situations.

The environment is a powerful influence even when its workings are subtle. To the extent that we view a person's reactions as unalterable and independent of the surrounding situation, we are prevented from identifying the conditions that produce and maintain his reactions. More important, we then fail to find, or even to look for, ways of altering these reactions (for example, by changing our own behavior).

*"I couldn't help it officer. I inherited a heavy foot from my father!"*

It should now be clear that behavior depends very much on the situation. We may be an important part of that situation. By accepting this fact, we then become aware of the large role we play in determining the behavior of any person with whom we interact. Along with this knowledge of our influence comes increased tolerance for the "flaws" we detect in others. How can we blame others for what we are, in part, responsible?

Thus, when we form unfavorable impressions of people, with-

out taking account of situational variables, we do them and ourselves an injustice. That first impression may lead us to reject
the person prematurely, not considering that he might have been
nervous, tired, uncomfortable, or that he might have seen us as
aloof, critical, or rejecting.

Perhaps assigning traits wouldn't be so damaging if all people
did was witness behavior and then give it a trait name. But rarely
do they stop there. Certain traits are seen as "belonging together." Thus, after affixing one label, the tendency is to fill in
the missing pieces to form a coherent whole. When the remaining pieces are given, as in the cold-warm illustration, the initial
label colors our perception of these characteristics. In the same
way, when the pieces are not supplied, the initial label will determine which ones will be chosen. Here, as is generally the case,
no other characteristics are given—they are supplied by the
viewer.

> Jerry prides himself on being a good judge of character. He amazes
> his friends by describing people in great detail after meeting them
> only briefly. His friends view him as something of a fortune-teller.
> While he does not consult the stars for his information, Jerry as-
> sumes that constellations of characteristics are often found to-
> gether. If the person he meets seems irritable or disagreeable, he
> will tell you he is jealous, willful, distrustful, competitive, stub-
> born. He will also describe in detail domestic, professional, and
> social situations in which these traits manifest themselves.

What if you had just been fired from your job and happened
to meet Jerry? Although it might be helpful to Jerry to package
people so concisely, albeit incorrectly, would you enjoy being
wrapped up and dismissed so lightly? How would you feel knowing nothing you could do would make Jerry change his description? Wouldn't you also feel that Jerry missed out by never getting to know you?

Under the title "bad," Jerry has assembled a catalogue of

traits. A person who falls into that category is, so to speak, "kicked downstairs," or relegated to an inferior position.

People also make the opposite error. A person who is seen initially as "good" may then be placed in a saintly role. At first glance it may seem fine to have such positive expectations: You are set to see the good. But the expectation is for perfection. And who can live up to that for long without tumbling from the pedestal?

Belief in traits and the attendant errors of judgment serve to erect barriers between people. A first impression, which should by definition be tentative, takes on an air of finality as the person is cast into a mold.

Can first impressions be changed? Usually they can. However, it is not an easy task. New actions are going to be interpreted in the old light.

Let's assume that a student does very well on the first exam of the semester. When he does poorly on the next test, what is the teacher likely to think? He'll think that the student is bright, but isn't exerting much effort. If the student did poorly on the first test and well on the second, however, he'd probably be seen as less bright, but a real worker.

It is difficult to undo that initial set. People are reluctant to admit error. Unless the new evidence is overpowering, they won't. The best way to avoid this difficulty is, of course, to create a positive impression from the start.

### How to Prevent or Change Negative Impressions

We said before that people are quick to make excuses to themselves when they behave foolishly, but tend to assign labels to others under similar conditions. This double standard occurs because we are well aware of the extenuating circumstances in our own case, but can't see them as easily for other people.

159

What can we do when we are the ones in danger of being un-fairly labelled? When the situational reasons for our behavior are not salient, it is possible to make them so. We can call them to the other person's attention ourselves.

> "I'm sorry I'm so slow today. I didn't get much sleep last night."

> "I hurt my wrist yesterday, so I'm all thumbs today. I'll pay for the cleaning."

> "I hope you didn't misinterpret that. We always tease each other that way. Some people become alarmed when they witness us in action because they take it too seriously."

> "That may have appeared hypocritical. I know I told him that I didn't know her very well when in fact I do. But I wanted her to succeed on her own merits rather than on my influence."

As you can see, we are suggesting the use of the disclaimer as a way of preventing or changing negative impressions. The other person may have little information on which to base his judgment. Therefore, it is important to make sure that this information is accurate. The disclaimer dispels the obvious misinterpretation by shifting the focus to the situational determinants of your seem-ingly inappropriate action.

Another approach to establishing that favorable impression is to take a questionable characteristic and treat it as an asset rather than a liability.

Although the following story is concerned with a characteris-tic on which you are not likely to be evaluated, it provides a good illustration of this point:

> Wanda is about 5'2" tall and of slight build. While her figure is quite good, there is one feature she has difficulty accepting—her feet. To her mind, they are unusually fat. The most painful ex-perience for her is to walk into a shoe store and not be able to fit into three-quarters of the shoes she tries on. She feels like Cin-derella's oversized sisters struggling to force their way into the tiny glass slipper. She expresses her dismay by lamenting: "Some-

times when I look down, I'd swear I had six toes on each foot."

A close friend of the authors also has unusually wide feet for a person of her size. However, here we see an entirely different situation. If someone happens to comment on the phenomenon, she is quick to turn their scorn to envy. She points out, quite convincingly, the adaptiveness of her well-endowed, "functional feet": They can walk for miles without getting tired, stand on long lines without aching, and break in shoes without hurting.

Our friend has done it in the same way that doctors made sloppy handwriting a mark of distinction—or that some professors have made absent-mindedness a sign of concern with weightier matters. They have all taken what might be viewed as handicaps and have confidently relabelled them as virtues. The viewer leaves the situation impressed and even somewhat envious.

People often worry about doing stupid things that will spoil the impression they are trying to create. You're on an interview —you slip and make a grammatical error, put your foot in your mouth, show your nervousness, or drop cigarette ashes on the rug. After you've committed one of these errors, you sit in dread that it was observed by the other person.

If indeed he has witnessed your faux pas, he probably is thinking what you're afraid he's thinking—that you're uneducated, insecure, unpolished, or clumsy. He may view your behavior as indicative of the kind of person you are, making little allowance for the stressfulness of the situation. Or he may be embarrassed for you and feel uncomfortable.

Oddly enough, the favorable impression is easily rescued by pointing out the error yourself and perhaps joking about it. Why does this work? Prior to your admission, the person is looking down on you from a "I-know-something-you-think-I-don't-know" position. After your announcement, you become a competent person who has committed a common error, rather than a common error who is trying to pass as a competent person. The fact that you've commented on your behavior lets the person know that the mistake is not typical of you—also that you know yourself and are confident enough to admit error. Finally, you demonstrate your ability to handle what might be seen as a difficult situation.

Suppose you have been harshly labelled and feel that you've changed enough so that your behavior no longer merits that description. What can you do? You can just continue behaving in this way in the hope that the other person will pick up on it and change his mind. But as you know, we usually advocate a more direct approach.

Once again this involves an open statement of what you believe to be the case. This amounts to telling the other person, "Look, I've changed. It's not fair to keep evaluating me in the old light." Invite him to test you out. Ask him to give you the opportunity to prove him wrong. You might point out that he wins either way—either you are no longer doing the thing that annoys him, or he has the satisfaction of being right.

But don't expect instant success. Be prepared for his lingering skepticism even after your first demonstration. Since you did behave in that way before, you really can't blame him for thinking that you'll continue behaving that way in the same situation now or in the future.

It can get pretty frustrating. You're trying very hard to show you've changed—maybe to please that person—and he just won't acknowledge it. You might be tempted to say it's not worth it—that you might as well do what you're being blamed for anyway.

Be patient.

A few more demonstrations, carefully pointed out, will probably be enough to win you a concession.

What if you feel you didn't merit that harsh label in the first place? Perhaps your behavior was misunderstood, and you don't wish to keep paying for it. In the same way, you can provide a statement of, and evidence for, the truth, along with a "You know, I see how you might have thought that."

Cheryl has asked Ernie to come shopping with her for a few minutes before they go to the movies. He reluctantly agrees. She then drags him to a huge department store where she soon becomes intrigued with all the latest apparel. She goes through the racks picking out *all* the appropriate articles to try on.

In the meantime, he is entertaining himself by examining the different pipes and tobacco nearby. After he is no longer amused he stations himself outside of the dressing room and waits. She thinks he's still wandering around the men's department, so she can take a few more minutes making her decisions. Becoming so engrossed in the activity, Cheryl loses track of the time. When she finally emerges from the dressing room she meets one furious Ernie. It seems she shopped right through the first part of the main feature and they can't wait for the second showing because they have to get up early next day to go to work.

Ernie's main argument is that Cheryl is selfish. He says she took the time because she wasn't hot on the movie in the first place. Because he started yelling at her, she didn't take the chance to express her agreement about her error. Since she did apologize later on the way home, he forgave her, although he was not going to forget.

People don't usually remember details of another person's behavior unless they are glaring. Thus all the attempts Cheryl made to change Ernie's mind went unnoticed. However, three weeks later when she kept him waiting for a luncheon engagement, he noticed again. Although he is not yelling this time, he does mention that she was thoughtless. She is enraged, for she has a perfectly good reason for being late and, in her words, she has been trying hard to please that ingrate all month. Instead of exploding, she convinces herself to take another approach.

"Ernie, I know I was selfish when I lost track of the time and we missed that movie, but since then I've been trying not to make the same mistake again. It becomes very frustrating, though, when you don't notice anything but my errors—especially today when it was out of my hands. Would you agree to make some acknowledge-ment when I don't do what you accuse me of doing. Otherwise, it's easy to forget, and then you end up thinking I'm something that I'm not."

"Sure honey," Ernie replies, chucking to himself that it's just a matter of time until she'll do it again. "Now what shall we have for lunch?"

Cheryl smiles back, thinking to herself that he may be humoring her now, but she'll have the last laugh, and answers, "A cheese-burger."

Since people's behavior has the potential to change from time to time and place to place, assigning traits is an inaccurate way of assessing individuals. Moreover, it can be harmful because it prevents us from looking at and understanding the total picture.

After accepting situational variables as important influences on behavior, you may still be left with an unanswered question. Does an emphasis on the power of situational variables do an injustice to man as a complex being? If anything, it is the "trait" position which belittles man's potential for complex, subtle, and varying behavior. By burdening him with fixed, internal charac-teristics it implies that he has a limited capacity for variability and change.

We can now give a definitive answer to one of the questions posed earlier: What's in a name? Plenty.

# EIGHT

# Give and Let Give

## YOU AND OTHERS

In all our discussions so far, you have been the main concern. We have demonstrated how an understanding of psychological principles can further your own happiness, your self-concept, your control, your persuasiveness, and so on. By this point you should be happy and self-confident enough to think seriously about others. Here we will be concerned with *others*—their happiness and their self-concept—and what you can do to promote them. No, we don't just mean by giving them the first seven chapters.

Throughout the book we have tried to demonstrate your influence over situations. While we've focused on the consequences of your actions for your own welfare, we have by no means neglected to consider the side effects they may have for others. We have pointed out many approaches which, if implemented properly, allow you to achieve your goals at nobody else's expense. In fact, many of these approaches allow other people to save face, feel magnanimous, and increase their self-esteem.

Now we would like to shift the focus from you to those other people. The goal will be explicitly to enhance that other person's satisfaction with himself and his interpersonal relationships.

Why should you be so concerned with other people now that you know how to "make it on your own"? Because other people are an integral part of your life—their happiness is affected by, and affects, you directly. Whenever you interact with another person, there is a chance that your actions and statements will go through a stage of interpretation. The more meaningful your interaction is to that person, the more likely this becomes. The interpretation he makes may result in encouragement or discouragement for him. Since you have the capacity to lead his thoughts in either direction, we see it as part of your responsibility to aim them and keep them on the track you initially intended.

What about "doing your own thing" where it's "every man for himself"? To the extent that this current emphasis on self-fulfillment has spurred people to realize their potential, all is well and good. But when that view is coupled with "If he doesn't understand, well that's *his* problem," it may reflect a problem on the part of the person making the assertion.

People who are unconcerned about the feelings of others are generally unhappy about themselves. In an effort to overcome feelings of discontent, they dwell on their own welfare. This perceived necessity for self-protection implies that there is a trade-off; the more attention they give to others, the less they have left for themselves, and the more vulnerable they become.

If these are your attitudes, once another person catches on to them, he is likely to accept them as the rules of the game—at least in terms of his interactions with you. By defining yourself as a competitor, his compliments become unlikely and his tact may be suspended. As long as you've declared that you're only looking out for yourself, who's left to protect him? The pity of this is that you then lose the chance to disconfirm your pessimism about yourself and the nature of the world. In other words, if you behave as though it's a dog-eat-dog world, that is just what it becomes for you.

With most people, however, failure to consider the other person results from carelessness rather than philosophy. "It didn't enter my mind that he would see it that way." You knew what you meant, and you assumed he would too. Such thoughtlessness does not stem from lack of concern. It generally results from a lack of awareness that you can predict how your actions are likely to affect others. When something is believed to be unpredictable, then any effort to exert control over that event is seen as futile. On the other hand, now that it is clear that certain reactions usually follow certain actions, it makes sense to take responsibility for the reactions your behavior occasions in others. Just as your successes and failures are not accidental, the pleasures and pains you give to others do not occur by chance.

Many of the psychological principles that we've suggested you put to use for your own benefit can be used to help out other people. Just as we've recommended ways for you to rid yourself of maladaptive cognitions and behavior, you can help others eliminate them from their repertoire. Here are just a few instances of how topics we've dealt with throughout the book can be used for the benefit of others.

## Control

We spoke of control initially as increasing desirable behavior or decreasing undesirable behavior through the use of rewards and punishments. You were in the driver's seat, determining the destination and planning the route. You may not have stopped to consider, however, the ways in which the same principles can be used explicitly for the other person's benefit.

Naturally, one thing you can do is to reward the person's actions as they more and more closely approximate the goal *he* has established for himself. While reaching the goal may bring him many rewards, your praise along the way may provide the motivation for him to sustain his efforts.

There are also less obvious ways in which your knowledge of these principles can be put to use for others. Assume, for the moment, that you've just asked your friend to go to the movies with you. At first he declined because of some important work he had to finish. But you had no qualms about convincing him. You might have been thinking that he can take care of himself and that if his obligation were important to his future he would, of course, decline—no matter what attempts you made. You were assuming that if the rewards working would bring him were greater than the rewards provided by your company and the movie, he could not be swayed. But was this way of thinking fair to him?

It is true that all rewards are not equally potent. The one that is strongest at a given moment will win out. But the power of any single reward may change as a function of *when* that reward may be obtained. A less attractive reward available immediately may be preferred to a more attractive one promised in the future. Thus if a person is working toward a future goal (tomorrow, next week, next year), and he accepts your offer of some form of immediate gratification, you are correct in assuming that at that time, he "wanted" the alternative you presented. However, in the long run, you have not done him a favor. It is not that your friend is weak, it is just that immediate rewards are strong.

While you are thinking of reward and punishment, you might keep in mind another major point. You do not reward or punish people. You reward or punish behavior. At first this may seem like a trivial point or merely an academic distinction. However, we cannot overemphasize its importance. The way you think about rewards and punishments influences the way you use them and the impact they have on the recipient. You might ask what difference does it really make if, after a child has done something wrong, you tell him "You're a bad boy" vs. "You did a bad thing"?

The difference it makes is in the child's image of himself. A bad boy is one who does bad things by nature. Even if he never performs that act again, it may not be clear to him that he is no longer bad. But by telling a child that he did a bad thing, you make clear the relationship between his actions and their consequences. Thus if he no longer performs that act, he no longer receives that punishment—his self-esteem is not in question. Similarly, in speaking to other adults, there is a great difference between calling someone stupid and telling him he's done a stupid thing. Smart people can do stupid things. Thus you have left open the possibility that you still think highly of him. In the other case, you've made a somewhat definitive assessment of his intelligence, in both your eyes and his own.

Another difference this distinction makes is in the strength of your reactions. It is surprising how much easier it is to become furious at a "bad" person than it is to become furious at a person who has done a bad thing. In a sense, the "bad" person is seen as deserving a much more severe punishment.

The child brought up on a diet of consistently rewarded and punished *behavior* grows into the adult who perceives his control over the environment. He has learned the relationship between his actions and their outcomes. He realizes that successes and failures are neither predetermined nor ruled by chance. They are a function of his efforts.

## Self-Concept

The closer you are to a person, the more responsibility you have for that person's self-concept and, consequently, his happiness. You are in the position to provide the support and reassurance that is necessary for his personal security.

It is unfortunate, then, that this kind of support and reassurance is rarely verbalized. When people are close, it is all supposed to be understood. "S(he) knows the way I feel; I don't have to state the obvious." However, the obvious becomes obscured over time. Statements of affection taper off, compliments become scarce, and apologies seem unnecessary—they are supposed to be understood.

Negatives, on the other hand, are not suspended—complaints and criticism have to be pointed out because they convey "real" information. In fact, it is often these negatives that people mistakenly see as the hallmarks of an open, honest relationship.

The result is an insidious imbalance. Positive thoughts and feelings are not conveyed because it seems unnecessary. Negative thoughts and feelings are conveyed because they provide valuable information. Since a person's self-concept is largely dependent upon external feedback, it is easy for the positive to be called into question in the absence of any statements to the contrary.

### Directed Thinking

Does an honest statement have to be a blunt one? There must have been times when you had to deliver difficult information—difficult because it was likely to hurt the other person. But since his pain was seen as inevitable, you probably focused on when you were going to break the news instead of how. Then, once you said what you felt you had to say, it was up to the other person to adjust to it. Your responsibility had ended.

Again, you might say that the relationship was such that the person would understand. Or, you might say that if the person were thinking positively, he could handle the situation with no help from you.

But why should you put him in the position of having to explain to himself why you had no choice, how much it must bother you, that you still think highly of him, that you can still be counted on, etc.?

By not considering *what* you should say and *how* you should say it, you put the other person in the position of having to interpret your statements for you. And he'll have to do a bit of interpreting to reconcile such inconsistent thoughts as "He's supposed to care about me" and "He's disappointed me."

There are ways of communicating difficult information so as to spare the other person's feelings and self-respect. That is, you can direct his thinking to more positive interpretations by anticipating how he might read the worst into your statements and actions. For example, suppose you had to fire someone. Instead of blurting out your "honest" statement, you might direct his thinking to less painful, though equally honest, considerations. You could point out how his talents are better suited for something else, rather than how his incompetence is not welcome here, or you could question the efforts he's devoted to the job rather than the ability he possesses.

In the process of considering *how* you should relate difficult information, it might be wise, in some cases, to question *whether you should convey it at all*. If it serves no other purpose than relieving your conscience, perhaps you should reconsider. Ask yourself how the other person will gain as a result of having this knowledge. If he will suffer more than he will benefit, then you might decide to keep it to yourself.

### Requests

Just as friends have a responsibility to do favors for each other when they're needed, they have a responsibility for the type of favor they ask of each other. People generally like to do whatever they can for the people they feel close to, but there is a limit on what they should be asked to do.

Making an unreasonable request of a person puts him in an extremely awkward position. He either has to turn you down and feel like a crumb or comply with something that may cause him great inconvenience. He may resent you as well if he thinks you are taking advantage of him, or that this is something you should, by all rights, be doing for yourself. While in any friendship people should feel free to ask favors, those favors should be carefully considered to make sure they are within the bounds of reason.

Does this mean that you should only ask favors when you're desperate? No. If you never ask favors of people they will be more hesitant to make requests of you. At first, this may seem like a good thing. However, what it really means is that you're keeping the relationship at a distance. If a person doesn't feel free to turn to you in need, then he can't define you as a friend —although you may be more than willing to help him out.

What about the case in which a person offers to do a favor for you? Some people decline because they don't want to put the person out or because they don't want to feel "obligated." But in most cases the person wouldn't offer if doing this thing for you didn't bring him some kind of pleasure. As for obligating—it is insulting of you to assume that he's being generous because he wants something in return.

When you never *ask* favors of people, you keep them at a distance; when you habitually refuse the favors they *offer*, it is as though you are pushing them away.

### Involvement

Sometimes a lower level of involvement allows you greater insight into another person's situation. Since you are viewing his problem from a distance you may have a better perspective. From this vantage point you may be able to find and point out the positive aspects that his involvement has prevented him from discovering.

There are, however, times when this low level of involvement can keep you from understanding what he is actually going through. Suppose someone shares his doubts about some future success with you. Your tendency is to rush in and quickly reassure him that of course he will succeed. After all, hasn't he always succeeded in the past? While you have every intention of building his confidence, this is not what happens. Instead he feels that you do not really understand his predicament. To him, this time is not like every other. Perhaps this time he did not prepare well enough, does not have the right people supporting him, does not feel up to what the task demands. Your positive remarks are seen as glib dismissals of his problem.

Isn't this a contradiction? We said before you should take the responsibility of pointing out the positive side and here we are saying that if you do point out the positive it might convey a lack of understanding. Clearly then some further explanation is necessary: your positive remarks will produce the intended effect only if they are preceded by a demonstration of empathy and concern. "I can understand why you're so worried. I probably would be also if I were in your shoes—but I think you have to keep in mind . . ." In this way you are appreciating the validity of his worries and at the same time are helping him to overcome them.

Similarly, if and when the person comes through successfully, you may say: "Of course you did it. Didn't I tell you you would?" This blasé attitude denies him the opportunity to cele-

*"Now let's drink to our leader, Herman Chandler, a molder of men, and inspiration to us all, and the man who paid for this dinner."*

brate what he views as a real accomplishment. That is, instead of sharing his surprise and delight, you accept his achievement as something that was a given and ignore all of his recent efforts.

Then there are times you may completely dampen the person's sense of achievement with perhaps well-meant, but disparaging comments.

"Guess what! I got a raise!"
"Well, it's about time they gave it to you."

"The coach said that soon I'll be good enough for the big league. Wouldn't that be exciting?"
"Yeah, that's nice. I think he's trying to build up the morale around here."

What happens when a person experiences failure? Aren't people then prone to be sympathetic? Not if they see the failure as having been deserved. If they view a half-hearted effort, carelessness, or stubbornness as the cause of the failure, their tendency is to moralize rather than sympathize. "Well, what did you expect?" To the person who is suffering, the immediate question isn't whether or not he brought this on himself, but rather, now that the damage is done, how can he handle it? And to this you are offering no solution.

Thus there are times when people seek out empathy—shared anxiety over an outcome, shared happiness over success, shared disappointment over failure—and if they do not receive it, then they cannot benefit from your subsequent advice.

## Labelling

Often when a person is self-conscious about a physical feature, an habitual behavior of theirs, or some faux pas they've committed, we sympathize, but see it basically as a problem they have to grapple with. If they bring it up we may try to reassure them that it's not as bad as all that—but if they don't believe us and persist in their foolishness, then what can we do?

174

Suppose we suspect that a person is ashamed of something, and we feel he is being ridiculous. We can help him to relabel it by complimenting it spontaneously—perhaps even before he brings it up himself. "You know, you really have a distinguished look. I think it's your aristocratic nose." "I love those little noises your stomach makes when you eat. I can tell it likes my cooking." While he may react by laughing and downgrading himself, he is sure to feel a lot more relaxed. Moreover, he doesn't have to wait in the dread that it will be "discovered" and secretly scorned.

What if a person you are with has committed a blunder and is obviously quite embarrassed? You can be the one to help him regain his composure. If, for example, he has dropped some food in his lap, you can relate a story about something you've done in the past that makes his action seem trivial by comparison. Or tell him that anything is excusable on Mondays. Or comment that the food is so bad that perhaps it's a better idea to drop it than eat it. Say anything that seems appropriate—any statement that will turn a tense moment into a light one, and shame into amusement.

In essence, we are suggesting that you do some personal politicking for the welfare of those around you.

Drawing by McCallister; © 1972 The New Yorker Magazine, Inc.

# REFERENCES

## Chapter II: Control

ADAMS, J. S. AND HOFFMAN, B. The frequency of self-reference statements as a function of generalized reinforcement. *Journal of Abnormal and Social Psychology*, 1960, 60, 384–89.

BALL, T. S. Issues and implications of operant conditioning: The reestablishment of social behavior. *Hospital and Community Psychiatry*, 1968, 19, 230–32.

BANDURA, A. Punishment revisited. *Journal of Consulting Psychology*, 1962, 26, 298–301.

BARON, R. M. Social reinforcement effects as a function of social reinforcement history. *Psychological Review*, 1966, 73, 527–39.

CATANIA, A. C. (ED.) *Contemporary research in operant behavior.* Glenview, Ill.: Scott Foresman, 1968.

CHEYNE, J. A. AND WALTERS, R. H. Intensity of punishment, timing of punishment and cognitive structure as determinants of response inhibition. *Journal of Experimental Child Psychology*, 1969, 7, 231–44.

ENDLER, N. S. The effects of verbal reinforcement on conformity and deviant behavior. *Journal of Social Psychology*, 1965, 66, 147–54.

FERSTER, C. B. AND SKINNER, B. F. *Schedules of reinforcement*. New York: Appleton-Century-Crofts, 1957.

GOLDIAMOND, I. Self-control procedures in personal behavior problems. *Psychological Reports*, 1965, 17, 851–68.

HARRIS, F. R., WOLF, M. M., AND BAER, D. M. Effects of adult social reinforcement on child behavior. *Young Children*, 1964, 20 (1).

LOGAN, F. A. AND WAGNER, A. R. *Reward and punishment*. Boston: Allyn & Bacon, 1965.

McNAIR, D. M. Reinforcement of verbal behavior. *Journal of Experimental Psychology*, 1957, 53, 40–46.

MISCHEL, W. AND EBBESON, E. B. Attention in delay of gratification. *Journal of Personality and Social Psychology*, 1970, 16, 329–37.

REISS, S. AND REDD, W. Generalization of the control of screaming behavior in an emotionally disturbed, retarded female. *Proceedings of the 78th Annual Convention of the American Psychological Association*, 1970, 741–42.

REYNOLDS, G. S. A *primer of operant conditioning*. Glenview, Ill.: Scott Foresman, 1968.

SKINNER, B. F. Freedom and the control of men. *American Scholar*, Winter 1955–1956, 25, 47–65.

SKINNER, B. F. *Science and human behavior*. New York: Macmillan, 1953.

STUART, R. B. Behavioral control of eating. *Behavior Research and Therapy*, 1967, 5, 357–65.

## Chapter III: Self-Concept

ARONSON, E. AND CARLSMITH, J. M. Performance expectancy as a determinant of actual performance. *Journal of Abnormal and Social Psychology*, 1962, 65, 178–183.

BERGER, E. M. The relation between expressed acceptance of self and expressed acceptance of others. *Journal of Abnormal and Social Psychology*, 1952, 47, 778–782.

DWECK, C. S. The role of expectations and attributions in the alleviation of learned helplessness in a problem-solving situation. Unpublished Doctoral Dissertation, Yale University, 1972.

DWECK, C. S. AND REPPUCCI, N. D. Learned helplessness and reinforcement responsibility in children. *Journal of Personality and Social Psychology*, 1972, in press.

ELLIS, A. *Reason and emotion in psychotherapy*. New York: Lyle Stuart, 1962.

FESTINGER, L. A theory of social comparison processes. *Human Relations*, 1954, 7, 117–40.

GERARD, H. B. AND RABBIE, J. M. Fear and social comparison. *Journal of Abnormal and Social Psychology*, 1961, 62, 586–92.

HARVEY, O. J. AND CLAPP, W. F. Hope, expectancy, and reactions to the unexpected. *Journal of Personality and Social Psychology*, 1965, 2, 45–52.

ISEN, A. M. Success, failure, attention, and reaction to others: The warm glow of success. *Journal of Personality and Social Psychology*, 1970, 15, 294–301.

MARACEK, J. The role of causal explanations in determining performance expectations and effort expenditure in maintaining a stable self-appraisal. Unpublished Doctoral Dissertation, Yale University, 1972.

SECORD, P. F., BACKMAN, C. W., AND EACHUS, H. T. Effects of imbalance in the self-concept on the perception of persons. *Journal of Abnormal and Social Psychology*, 1964, 68, 442–46.

SILVERMAN, I. Self-esteem and differential responsiveness to success and failure. *Journal of Abnormal and Social Psychology*, 1964, 69, 115–19.

## Chapter IV: Presenting Information

BERKOWITZ, L. AND GREEN, J. A. The stimulus qualities of the scapegoat. *Journal of Abnormal and Social Psychology*, 1962, 64, 293–301.

BERLYNE, D. E. Curiosity and exploration. *Science*, 1966, 153 (1), 25–33.

HOVLAND, C. I., JANIS, I. L., AND KELLEY, H. H. *Communication and persuasion*. New Haven: Yale University Press, 1953.

JANIS, I. L. AND KING, B. T. The influence of role-playing on opinion change. *Journal of Abnormal and Social Psychology*, 1954, 49, 211–18.

JANIS, I. L. AND MANN, L. Effectiveness of emotional role-playing in modifying smoking habits and attitudes. *Journal of Experimental Research in Personality*, 1965, 1, 84–90.

KAROUSE, D. E. AND GROSS, D. M. From specific acts to general dispositions. Unpublished Manuscript, University of California at Los Angeles, 1970.

McGUIRE, W. J. The effectiveness of supportive and refutational defenses in immunizing and restoring beliefs against persuasion. *Sociometry*, 1961, 24, 184–97.

McGUIRE, W. J. AND PAPAGEORGIS, D. The relative efficacy of various types of prior belief-defense in producing immunity against persuasion. *Journal of Abnormal and Social Psychology*, 1961, 62, 327–37.

MILLS, J. AND ARONSON, E. Opinion change as a function of the communicator's attractiveness and desire to influence. *Journal of Personality and Social Psychology*, 1965, 1 (2), 173–77.

WALSTER, E., ARONSON, E., AND ABRAHAMS, D. On increasing the persuasiveness of a low prestige communicator. *Journal of Experimental Social Psychology*, 1966, 2, 325–42.

## *Chapter V: Requests*

ABELSON, R. P., ARONSON, E., McGUIRE, W. J., NEWCOMB, T. M., ROSENBERG, M. J., AND TANNENBAUM, P. H. (eds.) *Theories of cognitive consistency: A sourcebook*. Chicago: Rand McNally, 1968.

BEM, D. J. Self-perception: An alternative interpretation of cognitive dissonance phenomena. *Psychological Review*, 1967, 74, 183–200.

BREHM, J. W. AND SENSENIG, J. Social influence as a function of attempted and implied usurpation of choice. *Journal of Personality and Social Psychology*, 1966, 4, 703–7.

BROWN, J. S. Gradients of approach and avoidance responses and their relation to level of motivation. *Journal of Comparative and Physiological Psychology*, 1948, 41, 450–65.

DARLEY, J. M. AND LATANE, B. Bystander intervention in emergencies: Diffusion of responsibility. *Journal of Personality and Social Psychology*, 1968, 8 (4), 377–83.

FESTINGER, L. AND CARLSMITH, J. M. Cognitive consequences of forced compliance. *Journal of Abnormal and Social Psychology*, 1959, 58, 203–10.

FREEDMAN, J. L. AND FRASER, S. C. Compliance without pressure: The foot-in-the-door technique. *Journal of Personality and Social Psychology*, 1966, 4, 195–202.

FREEDMAN, J. L. AND STEINBRUNER, J. D. Perceived choice and resistance to persuasion. *Journal of Abnormal and Social Psychology*, 1964, 68 (6), 678–81.

LANGER, E. J. AND ABELSON, R. P. How to succeed in getting help without really dying: The semantics of asking a favor. *Journal of Personality and Social Psychology*, 1972, 24, 26–33.

LATANE, B. AND DARLEY, J. M. Group inhibition of bystander intervention in emergencies. *Journal of Personality and Social Psychology*, 1968, 10 (3), 215–21.

LEVENTHAL, H., SINGER, R., AND JONES, S. Effects of fear and specificity on recommendation upon attitudes and behavior. *Journal of Personality and Social Psychology*, 1965, 2 (1), 20–29.

MILLER, N. E. Comments on theoretical models illustrated by the development of a theory of conflict behavior. *Journal of Personality*, 1951, 20, 82–100.

Rokeach, M. Long range experimental modification of values, attitudes and behavior. *American Psychologist*, 1971, 26, 453–59.

WORCHEL, S. AND BREHM, J. W. Effect of threats to attitudinal freedom as a function of agreement with the communicator. *Journal of Personality and Social Psychology*, 1970, 14, 18–22.

ZIMBARDO, P. G. The human choice: Individuation, reason and order versus deindividuation, impulse and chaos. *Nebraska Symposium on Motivation.* Lincoln: University of Nebraska Press, 1969.


## Chapter VI: Obtaining Information

ELLSWORTH, P. C. AND CARLSMITH, J. M. Effects of eye contact and verbal content on affective response to a dyadic interaction. *Journal of Personality and Social Psychology,* 1968, 10, 15–20.

MEHRABIAN, A. Significance of posture and position in the communication of attitude and status relationships. *Psychological Bulletin,* 1969, 71, 359–72.

MILGRIM, S. Behavioral study of obedience. *Journal of Abnormal and Social Psychology,* 1963, 67, 371–78.

ORNE, M. On the social psychology of the psychological experiment: With particular reference to demand characteristics and their implications. *American Psychologist,* 1962, 17, 776–83.

OSTRUM, T. M. Perspective as an intervening construct in the judgment of attitude statements. *Journal of Personality and Social Psychology,* 1966, 3, 135–44.

ROSENTHAL, R. On the social psychology of the psychological experiment: The experimenter's hypothesis as unintended determinant of experimental results. *American Scientist,* 1963, 51, 268–83.

ZILLMANN, D. Rhetorical elicitation of agreement in persuasion. *Journal of Personality and Social Psychology,* 1972, 21 (2), 159–65.


## Chapter VII: Impressions

ASCH, S. Forming impressions of personality. *Journal of Abnormal and Social Psychology,* 1946, 41, 258–90.

BROPHY, J. E. AND GOODE, T. L. Teachers' communication of differential expectations for children's classroom performance: Some behavioral data. *Journal of Educational Psychology,* 1970, 61, 365–74.

DORNBUSH, S. M., HASTORF, A. H., RICHARDSON, S. A., MUZZY, R. E.,

AND VREELAND, R. S. The perceiver and the perceived: Their relative influence on the categories of interpersonal cognition. *Journal of Personality and Social Psychology*, 1965, 1 (5), 434–40.

HASTORF, A. H. AND CANTRIL, H. They saw a game: A case study. *Journal of Abnormal and Social Psychology*, 1954, 49, 129–34.

HUGUENARD, T., SAGER, E. B., AND FERGUSON, L. W. Interview time, interview set, and interview outcome. *Perceptual and Motor Skills*, 1970, 31, 831–36.

KELLEY, H. H. The warm-cold variable in first impressions of persons. *Journal of Personality*, 1950, 18, 431–39.

LANGER, E. J. AND ABELSON, R. P. A job applicant by any other name: The effect of labels on clinician's assessments. (in press)

LERNER, M. J. Evaluation of performance as a function of performer's reward and attractiveness. *Journal of Personality and Social Psychology*, 1965, 1 (4), 355–60.

LERNER, M. J. AND SIMMONS, C. H. Observer's reaction to the "innocent victim": Compassion or rejection? *Journal of Personality and Social Psychology*, 1966, 4, 203–10.

MISCHEL, W. Continuity and change in personality. *American Psychologist*, 1969, 24, 1012–18.

MODIGLIANI, A. Embarrassment, facework, and eye contact: Testing a theory of embarrassment. *Journal of Personality and Social Psychology*, 1971, 17 (1), 15–24.

NISBETT, R. E., CAPUTO, C., LEGANT, P., AND MARACEK, J. Behavior as seen by the actor and as seen by the observer. *Journal of Personality and Social Psychology*, in press.

ROSENTHAL, R. AND JACOBSON, L. *Pygmalion in the classroom: Teacher expectancy and pupils' intellectual development.* New York: Holt, Rinehart & Winston, 1968.

TAYLOR, S. E. AND METEE, D. R. When similarity breeds contempt. *Journal of Personality and Social Psychology*, 1971, 20 (1), 75–81.

ULRICH, R. E., STACHNIK, T. J., AND STAINTON, N. R. Student acceptance of generalized personality interpretations. *Psychological Reports*, 1963, 13, 831–34.

WALSTER, E. Assignment of responsibility for an accident. *Journal of Personality and Social Psychology*, 1966, 3 (1), 73–79.

## *Chapter VIII: Others*

BESSELL, H. The content is the medium: The confidence is the message. *Readings in developmental psychology today*. Del Mar, Calif.: CRM, 1970.

JECKER, J. AND LANDY, D. Liking a person as a function of doing him a favour. *Human Relations*, 1969, 22 (4), 371–78.

LANGER, E., JANIS, I., AND WOLFER, J. The effect of a cognitive coping device and information on relieving preoperative stress (in preparation).

SCHOPLER, J. AND COMPERE, J. S. Effects of being kind or harsh to another on liking. *Journal of Personality and Social Psychology*, 1971, 20, 155–59.

# TOPICAL INDEX

191